The Gap

Simple Steps to Reclaim Your Health and Reverse Most Chronic Diseases

Pantea Kalhor

Reed Davis, Dr. Tara Scott,

Dr. Defne Nayman, Fiona Mao

Salena Rothenberger, Dr. Jordanna Quinn,

Christi Clemons Hoffman

Edited by Angela Curtis

https://acechoiceidea.com

Table of Content

Copyright

The Gap

ISBN-13: 978-1-7780351-0-4

https://acechoiceidea.com

AceChoice Publishing and Branding

This Book is Dedicated to

My husband, my best friend, my real support, and love of my life. His patience through this entire process and his kind support kept me inspired to accomplish my mission of sharing stories of hope and healing.

My Parents, my anchors, my shelters, and my safety.

My beautiful daughter who let me be her mother and feel the real depth of motherhood. Her birth changed my world and inspired me to continue advocating integrative medicine and mind-body connection modalities.

My authors who believed in me and supported me during the entire process of writing and publishing this book.

My readers who support me by reading my books and watching my podcasts. Through all the interviews with medical doctors, healers, and holistic medicine practitioners, I learned that life is so beautiful and worthy to live. A little shift in lifestyle can make a big difference in regaining our health to enjoy our life with less pain and more happy moments.

Pantea Kalhor March 1st, 2022

Other Books by Pantea Kalhor

1. Rules of Change for the Better: Real Stories and Your Guide to Tune-Up Your Mood and Transform Your Life to Reach Your Biggest Dreams
   https://therulesofchange.com

2. Naturally Conceived: How to Get Pregnant, Explain Unexplained Infertility and Prevent Miscarriages by Unleashing Your Reproductive Power Even Over 40!
   https://panteakalhor.com

3. PTSD Compass: Navigate Trauma to Triumph and Renew Your Life
   https://acechoiceidea.com/funnel/ptsd-compass

Foreword by Dr. Defne Nayman, MD, Anti-Aging, Functional, & Metabolic Medicine

The Gap, with its befitting name, is addressing the unerring gap between conventional medicine and true wellness.

As a conventionally trained MD who worked for years in a traditional medical practice, I personally experienced how conventional medicine fails to fill the gap when it comes to long term health, ending chronic symptoms and avoiding chronic illness. While conventional medicine does excel at acute care, I became frustrated trying to help people dealing with more and more chronic issues. I decided to seek out additional training in other forms of healing, including Mind-Body Medicine, and along the way, I met Pantea.

I am so grateful to Pantea for gathering experts in the wellness field to shed a light on the gaps in our current medical system and inspire practitioners like myself. Pantea's extensive podcasts and relentless discussions with wellness providers spearheaded this very book project, a brilliant compilation of perspectives that fosters awe and curiosity.

Sadly, we are simultaneously blessed and victimized by 21st-century living—we have all the conveniences of modern life and yet we are struggling more than ever with health issues. We all know someone who is suffering from the ailments of industrialized living.

There is no need to look far; maybe our loved ones or ourselves are already going through some form of a dis-ease process without the full manifestation of a chronic illness. The most common chronic illnesses such as diabetes, hypertension, heart disease, and cancer, all start with preceding metabolic states which are not addressed timely and effectively in the conventional medical model. It is a no-win situation when root causes are not addressed, and lifestyle is not prioritized, allowing symptoms like fatigue, stomach issues, weight gain, daily pain, etc. to spin out of control.

Only when we address our health on all levels (mind, body, and energy) and nourish all aspects of our beings can we stop the causes of chronic symptoms that are ignored in conventional medicine and so often lead to something far more serious.

As a practitioner who has finally found the sweet spot between western medicine and ancient eastern wisdom, I've experienced accelerated healing for myself and my patients dealing with chronic health complaints. Ancient wisdom and new modalities of assessing and achieving wellness are now being vetted more and more by modern medical professionals who can see their value and yearn to deliver a more complete care.

Our approach to well-being is starting to shift, little by little! It's not about managing illnesses anymore. Many of us providers are evolving and prioritizing prevention, optimized health, and wellness in all aspects of people's lives.

While our health care system is still lagging, it’s more important now than ever to be consistent in our message that we *need* a new approach. After all, “consistency carves canyons” as they say, and together with awareness, education, and taking initiative, we can shape the future of medicine.

Dr Defne Nayman

Feb 28, 2022

Foreword by Salena Rothenberger, Functional Medicine Practitioner

In 2014, when I sat by my oldest child in the pediatric ICU, I had no idea it would lead to connecting with health professionals who were on the same journey. For over 24 hours I didn't eat or sleep as my mind raced with how my child came to be in this state of health and what we could do to restore his body so that he was 'normal' once again. We spent over a year searching from coast to coast, but never seemed to reach the goal we were after until we learned of a different approach.

The GAP is a collection of the heart and soul of others who have been in the trenches searching for a way out. However, it's more than that. It is an extraordinary handbook of how they successfully navigated what seemed like an impassable gap. The reality is I had been looking for answers since the 1990s when I suffered with infertility and four miscarriages. Had I known about the hidden stressors that lead to dis-ease, or how much of an impact the simple task of breathing could have on my health, or how the foods we eat can work against us instead of healing us, I would have done things very differently. If only I had known that we can influence our genes, find solutions to my infertility & PCOS, and had someone who truly listened, I imagine my other four children would be with us today and my other two would not have to face chronic diseases.

However, would you and I be at this junction together had I not experienced these tragedies?

Pantea has once again done a brilliant job of uniting experts who have faced what seemed impossible and are now on missions to share how to get to the other side. It has been an honor and privilege to be part of this work. If you have been looking for answers only to be left feeling like you are alone, this book will provide a renewal of hope and connection that empowers the deepest part of your spirit so you, too, can bridge the gap.

Editorial Note

Once again, Pantea has created a valuable resource for all who want to find answers to their health issues. It's a collaboration of experts who started off as highly trained medical professionals that turned to natural, holistic practices to find the root causes of illness in their fields.

This book intrigued me as many years ago, I studied to be a naturopath. My health took a turn for the worse as I went through a messy divorce, and I was unable to continue. Since then, I have made it my life's mission to learn how my body was created and how I could improve my health.

My most exciting discovery was proof of what I'd known all along. Our bodies have the ability to heal themselves of most ailments. Each trauma and emotion experienced over a lifetime can lead to physical ailments. There really is a mind and body connection. Some treatments are quick fixes, others take time, persistence, sometimes a little medical intervention, and an open mind.

If you want to learn more about the secrets to longevity and lifestyle medicine, read on, dear one. Inside, you will find hope as you learn about the incredible results you too can achieve naturally. There are in-depth instructions and links to further studies on the hidden causes of infertility, chronic children's disease, and immune disease. You will learn about breath work, your body's energy system, and how you can improve your cellular health.

These experts have gone right to the grass roots of the diseases and afflictions in their fields. It's an extraordinary read and I recommend it to anyone who wants to learn more about their remarkable bodies and find a more peaceful and pain-free way to live. We truly can perish from a lack of knowledge.

If you need a light of hope to shine into the darkness of your ailment and disability, this book is for you. It will illuminate your path to a healthier and more enjoyable life. I've learned so much from this book and experienced remarkable results using these treatments. You can too.

So, keep reading, dear warrior. Fight for your health. Your freedom is near.

Angela

Contact me at: info@kinandkingdomsbooks.com

Praise For “The Gap”

Eye-opening

From breathwork to functional medicine, to genetics and energy, the experts in this book look at all aspects of health for a full picture of *The Gap* between Western and alternative medicine. It is for anyone on a difficult health journey seeking to look at the broader picture.

Leslie Lindsey Davis, author of "You Can't Eat Love"

This will change your life!!

This book is phenomenal! It is useful, informative, and written well. If I can understand it well enough to be able to apply to my life, anyone can. Thank you to all the authors!

Amazon reader

No band aids, this will help you find and heal the root cause of disease

A comprehensive read about getting to the root cause of dis-ease and ways to heal our body, mind, and spirit. This is valuable information that should be taught to our children and doctors. Love this book!

Amazon reader

An excellent assembly of expert views on wholistic wellness

This book is a great resource for people looking to learn and understand beyond conventional medicine. The authors have brought their knowledge and wisdom in a way unparalleled to any other book on the subject of wellness. There is an abundance of information and there are great perspectives that relate to just about anyone. While there is an emphasis on chronic symptoms and illnesses, preventive measures are also highlighted. It is an easy and beautiful read. I highly recommend it for people wanting to learn more about keeping their mind and body in good health!

Susan Jagannath, author of Travel and Adventure books: The Valley of Flowers, Chasing Himalayan Dreams; The Camino Ingles.

The missing link in your health

I just love Pantea's unique and insightful contributions to health and wellbeing, so I grabbed this book as soon as I saw she had created a collection of invaluable tips that address the gap between medicine and lifestyle. From Genes, to breathe, diet and into the very bones of your body, there is something significant to learn that can make you healthier, happier and wiser.

The short chapters focussed on a single issue make this book a quick read, and especially at this time when we all need to take responsibility for our health and that of our families. If you have any form of chronic ailment, there are ideas in this book that will help you.

Good and vital information for one's health

A good, well-written collection of information pertaining to tools and information necessary to attain and maintain optimal health. The writer knows her work well and provides useful tools that anyone can apply to their lives.

Disclaimer

The Gap is the collective work of medical doctors, a nurse practitioner, functional medicine, and holistic medicine practitioners. They have shared their solutions in treating their own health crises or what have worked for them in treating their patients.

The authors and publisher do not intend to diagnose, cure, treat, or prevent any condition or disease. Before you begin any healthcare program, or change your lifestyle, you should consult your physician or another licensed healthcare practitioner to choose the right tool.

This book is not intended as a substitute for consultation with a licensed healthcare practitioner, such as your physician.

The Gap provides content related to physical and/or mental health issues. As such, use of this book implies your acceptance of this disclaimer.

Introduction

I am sitting in the emergency room connected to an oxygen tank. My 2-year-old daughter is with her dad in the children's ward. She just started going to daycare and now gets sick easily and struggles with different viruses.

Last night, she had croup, a viral infection that causes inflammation and swelling in the lining of the windpipe and voice box. She coughed and wheezed as she breathed. We immediately took her to the hospital. They kept us in overnight.

I didn't feel right either. My chest was tightening, and my breath was short. My husband had a full day of work and looked tired and very overwhelmed with worry and a lack of sleep. I couldn't stop coughing and couldn't catch my breath.

"Are you ok?" he asked, anxiously grasping my hand. I tried to catch my breath and could barely reply. I gathered what energy I had to respond.

"I need to go to the emergency room," I mumbled. That wasn't the first time I ended up in the emergency room. I knew this shortness of breath would eventually lead me there.

"I can't leave our daughter here," he said. "We'll ask someone for help."

"Don't worry," I said. "I can handle it." I waved my hand, nodded my head, and took another breath, knowing I'd have to keep it short.

"I will go by myself." I pointed at my daughter. "Please take care of her." I blew her a kiss, and she looked back at me as if shocked I was leaving her. Leaving them both there was extremely difficult. I rushed down to the emergency room. They did the registration work and immediately connected me to the oxygen tank. My husband called half an hour later. I removed the mask to answer his call.

"I am connected to the oxygen tank. Is everything fine?" I could hear my daughter crying, asking for her mom.

"She is very restless and panicked, not seeing you around. I just wanted her to hear your voice." He put the phone to her ear.

"Hi, Sweety. Mommy is here. Be a good girl. I will be back soon."

She suddenly stopped crying, and I heard her dad trying to distract her by singing and playing.

I couldn't swallow my grudge. I didn't want to be anywhere but by my baby girl's side. She needed my attention. I was determined that when I got out of the emergency room, I was going to hold her tightly and tell her everything was going to be ok. I wanted to be healthy and live a long life so I could see her grow up. I just wanted to take care of her.

It's so scary to discover you can't rely on your lungs to breathe. I suffered for years with asthma. I longed to take a deep and clean breath without wheezing and without having to use a puffer and an oxygen tank.

It was asthma that initiated my journey to holistic body recovery. While visiting an acupuncturist during my fertility journey, I discovered asthma was one of the blockers in my reproductive system. As soon as I had my baby girl, I gave more attention to integrative medicine.

I interviewed amazing medical doctors, functional and holistic medicine practitioners, PTSD (Post Traumatic Stress Disorder) coaches, and psychotherapists in over 175 episodes on my podcast. It encouraged me to be an advocate for integrative medicine and to study functional medicine. Finding this new world of possibilities and hearing real stories from medical doctors and health care professionals was so promising. I knew at bottom of my heart that it was also going to work for me.

I wanted to go back to the way I had been and dreamed of running my daily tasks comfortably without having to think about my breath. I wanted to resume swimming 80 laps of the 25-meter pool without trouble inhaling. Health is the best gift we have, and we can never replace it with anything else. We need to protect this treasure and improve its functionality.

I learned so much, like how every piece of our body is related to each other and how eliminating the symptoms doesn't necessarily remove the root cause of our discomfort. I discovered it is possible to improve our health and find healing opportunities in our bodies, even if we've suffered from chronic pain for a long time.

Why Did I Write This Book?

The power of integrative medicine has not been well accepted by the public yet. Most people just look for fast and temporary relief by using medication. Some fixes need immediate medical intervention like heart surgeries and broken legs, but some pain stays with us for years and builds up overtime.

The root cause of many chronic diseases may originate from fear, emotional trauma, childhood abuse, loss, and abandonment. Or it may have been hidden behind other physical layers. In my two previous books, I tried to talk more about root causes of unexplained infertility and how Post Traumatic Stress Disorder can affect mental and physical health.

In this book, I talk more about chronic disease. I was fortunate to have amazing experts in this collection. I selected from the best and felt the urge to share their stories and practical advice with others, to offer hope to those who have suffered from chronic pain for years. The experts have proven evidence that integrative medicine works. They applied it to their own practices and had great success.

The Gap highlights the power of integrative medicine. We talk about choosing the right lifestyle and diet, the secrets of longevity, the right breath technique for optimal health, and reversing autoimmune and children's chronic disease.

We also discuss the power of orthopedic medicine and highlight the root causes of fertility issues. The last chapter underlines the importance of energy work on our body, and it clarifies how emotional discomfort can cause disease. It also explains how we are not only a physical body, but we have a soul and energy.

Who Should Read This Book?

If you want to continue feeling exhausted and live a life with chronic pain, then you shouldn't bother reading this book. But if you are a warrior and tired of taking medication to subside the pain and would like to fight for your health, find the root cause of your problem and have a happier and pain-free quality of life, then keep reading.

This book is a small yet valuable portion of all my interviews in over 175 episodes on my YouTube channel. They are all appraised and highly respected professionals who dedicate their lives to saving others. They all believe in mind-body connection healing modalities. I hope these stories and solutions will help you find your own customized health plan and show you the real value of integrative medicine.

CHAPTER 1

Lifestyle Medicine is Good for All That Ails You

By Reed Davis, Founder of FDN, a board-certified Holistic Health Practitioner (HHP) and expert in functional lab testing and natural protocols

In the 90s I was saving the planet, working as an environmental paralegal and conservationist. That means cleaning up our air, land, and water, and saving the birds, trees, and bees and so on. It was obvious the environment was destroying many of these things. One day while riding my motorcycle out in the desert, I had a thought.

"If the environment is so harsh on the rest of the planet, what's it doing to people, including me?" That was over twenty years ago. From then on, I turned my attention to helping people. I didn't want anything to sneak up on me either, so I changed careers and went to work in a wellness center in Southern California. They hired me to run the business, but I soon became a clinical nutritionist, a personal fitness trainer, and eventually, the Health Director.

After speaking with just handful of patients, it became crystal clear that people were stuck in a cycle of trial and error. Almost everyone walking into the office had a similar story. It really bothered me when they said they had already seen five or more practitioners, some even eight or ten practitioners, but they still had their original complaints.

Personally, I never had any real health challenges other than getting banged up in football, martial arts, surfing, skiing, and motorcycle riding (and one or two bar fights, but that's another story). I guess you could say I have a well-used body. But I didn't know how bad our medical system was until I noticed that almost everyone coming into our office with chronic stress-related problems was caught in this cycle of trial and error. They were desperately searching for someone who could identify exactly what was wrong with them so they could fix it permanently instead of just chasing the symptoms. Again, I was out riding my bike one day when another thought occurred to me

"Here I am on my bike, totally free and healthy, and these folks are trapped like rats in a maze. What a ripoff!"

As naïve as it sounds (and it was), I told myself I was going to be the last person they would need to see. I didn't know how, but I knew these people were putting control of their health in the wrong hands. They needed to take back the control, and I determined I was going to help. That was the day everything changed.

“We’re going to figure this thing out and fix it permanently instead of just going from one practitioner to the next, hoping for relief,” I started telling my clients.

“You’ve had this problem for years; you’ve tried different therapies, and diets, and every kind of supplement and modality. Yet here you are still searching. Your doctors only offer drugs and surgery because that’s all they have to work with.”

The response was amazing. I believed then, as I do know, people are too smart these days to just chase the symptoms and resort to drugs and surgery. They want real answers.

Like the little train that could, I started chugging away, really believing there was a solution and that I could make a difference. Fortunately, our patients were willing to try. We had access to all the alternative lab work of the day and I was a voracious worker. The thought that it can’t be done never entered my mind.

I reviewed thousands of lab reports for thousands of people and while I had very good mentoring at the time, I made my own observations about who got better and who didn’t. It should be no surprise to any reader that those working closest to the underlying cause got the best results. But what is not so intuitive, I soon realized, was that people with the same symptoms could have completely different underlying causes or conditions. That led to me coining the phrase, Metabolic Chaos®.

What is Metabolic Chaos®?

A lady came into our office and the look on her face told me she was very unhappy. She was a chiropractic patient at our center and had not started working with me yet. I escorted her back to a treatment room.

"What's wrong Susan? You don't seem to be yourself today?" I asked.

"Well, it's these 40 pounds of extra weight. I can't stand it," she said.

"Well, what are we going to do about it?" I said in my most encouraging voice.

"There is nothing I can do about it," she said, wincing.

"I've been on medication for the hives for two years and it makes me fat. I visited my doctor the other day and told him I was very unhappy with this extra weight. He told me I had a choice: you can be fat, or you can have the hives, take your pick. I told him that was very depressing, and he replied that he'd be happy to write me a prescription for anti-depressants!"

Thank goodness she passed on the antidepressants, but the look on her face was quite hopeless.

"Susan, did you ever try to find out what was causing the hives?" I asked, trying to look at her nonchalantly. Her head snapped around with a look I'll never forget.

"What do you mean?" That instant look of hope was so endearing, and I knew I had to help her. I knew I could help her.

After her appointment with the chiropractor, I sent her home with a couple of test kits and in a very short period; we had some clues about what was causing or triggering her unwanted and tormenting condition. Among other healing opportunities, we identified some foods that were contributing to the Metabolic Chaos®. The results were almost immediate. Within just a couple weeks of strict avoidance, she saw real change.

"Reed, I called my doctor and told him I was off the medication. And you know what else? For two years I haven't been able to take a hot shower or work out to the point of perspiration because, even on the medication, I'd still get the hives.

"Well, this weekend I not only went to the gym and worked up a sweat, but I went home and took a hot shower. It was so wonderful, thank you." Just a few short weeks later, she told me she'd lost 13 lbs and was on the road to her old self. We were both thrilled and somewhat amazed. But Metabolic Chaos® is a fickle mistress.

Why is Metabolic Chaos® So Important?

Soon after Susan's miracle occurred, another person came to the office with a similar problem. I thought I knew the answer and exactly what to do. But the same tests barely helped, if at all. In Susan's case, we had quickly identified key contributors to Metabolic Chaos®. In the other case, we had not (not yet). As you will see, it's not called chaos for nothing.

In another case, a lady was coming in for Chiro care, as well as my services for hormonal complaints.

"Do you work with children?" she asked. Twenty years ago, I had never reviewed labs for a kid. I had, however, helped raise four of them and had been a youth football coach for 15-years.

"Sure, I work with kids," I said. "What's going on?" She explained that her 9-year-old son was having problems at school, and she was told by a teacher or administrator that her son had ADHD. They suggested he should be on medication to improve his behavior. She was very distraught. I, always the hero, asked her, "Do you think your son has a medication deficiency?" We both laughed about that, but she did a couple of tests on the young man. Sure enough, within a two-week period, after we changed his diet, sleep and exercise schedule, the change in him was significant enough for the principal of the school to track me down.

"What did you put Billy on?" He asked. To him, the boy's complete turnaround in behavior seemed like a miracle.

We found an underlying contributor to the neurological problems and imbalances and those causing his inability to pay attention and annoy the other kids. I have plenty to say about school-house diagnosis, but that is for other time. All we did was sort out Metabolic Chaos®.

Sorting Out Metabolic Chaos®

Metabolic Chaos® is a state that exists when there are multiple causal factors at work. Sometimes they're far upstream from where the symptoms appear, or where the disease process is manifesting in the body. These imbalances or dysfunctions are influencing one another, making it almost impossible to identify, except by indirect measurement.

So, instead of looking for one marker or dot that would allow a doctor to make a diagnosis, I learned to identify multiple indicators that would allow me to connect the dots. The good news is, I have an eye for recognizing patterns.

Resolving Metabolic Chaos® became my one concern. Since I wasn't a physician, I wasn't bound to the same system or algorithm that their licensure demands of them. Except for a few, doctors are still handcuffed to the strict 'diagnosis and treatment' model of care.

Thankfully, I had the freedom to review all kinds of lab work and learned to identify as many 'healing opportunities' as possible for an individual. The patterns I recognized led to knowing which labs would most likely help sort out their Metabolic Chaos®.

Sorting out Metabolic Chaos® means identifying as many imbalances, dysfunctions, and healing opportunities as possible. Then, of course, applying the general principles of health building, instead of just treating the paper.

Often, physicians look at an out-of-range marker, provide a diagnosis (label) and then prescribe an agent (drug) to move the needle on that marker. In our world, we call that treating the paper. We must look at the lab data (mostly non-standard lab work) only to identify healing opportunities or what's truly wrong with a person. That's what we routinely teach in our program for health practitioners.

So, the healing opportunities appear when we review enough lab data and correlate it with an individual and how they are showing up. It's amazing how the data on functional lab work can explain exactly why a person feels the way they do. Clients are astonished at how conditions that have baffled other practitioners fall neatly into line and point the finger at exactly what is needed to resolve the problem.

Once healing opportunities are identified, we don't just get out the prescription pad or provide a list of supplements. If only it were that easy. Rather, over the years, we've developed a complete lifestyle program. It's a holistic program that does not treat anything specifically but treats everything non-specifically. So, every cell, every tissue, every organ, every system gets the benefit of these changes we make in behavior. It is truly a holistic, epigenetic lifestyle, environment, and behavior program.

We run the labs and we look for healing opportunities in 6 specific areas. If you identify a whole cluster of the most important healing opportunities, then customize and apply the general principles of health building to that person, (there are five major ones), his/her body responds, and he/she gets better.

We have been developing this approach by working with our clients for over 20 years. In 2008, the pressure to teach others became so great that I finally put a 2-day workshop together and invited a few people to attend. Here again, the response was extraordinary.

Practitioners who had been struggling for years to handle difficult cases saw the light. That weekend became the foundation for what is now one of the most respected training programs in the world–Functional Diagnostic Nutrition® (FDN). Now, others can do what we have done successfully in the Southern California office, working with thousands of people. It just works, so we want to spread the love around the world.

Intelligence Gathering: Why the Diagnosis and Treatment Model Fails in Chronic Stress-related Conditions

I offer no medical diagnosis for anything, ever. To that endeavor, we grant licensed physicians a complete monopoly. People with persistent health problems have had enough diagnoses. It's critical to know what the upstream healing opportunities are. Can we neutralize or remove a chronic stressor? Can we correct a deficiency, an imbalance, or improve whatever dysfunction is upstream and filtering down to create the chaos?

Sometimes it's an easy fix when you know what labs to look at. But occasionally, there are multiple causal factors that bounce into each other here and there. They're all crashing into one another, having an often-unmeasurable effect. It's only possible to sort it all out if you have a good system. But if you think running one lab will do it, I'm here to tell you it's unlikely at best.

For example, take a patient who is given a brief quiz about symptoms, then told "It sounds like thyroid." After the practitioner has checked their thyroid levels, he pats himself on the back and proclaims, "Yep, found your problem. It's low thyroid."

Then, of course, out comes the prescription pad, and it becomes all about dosage and frequency. The patient is told to come back in three months, to have their levels checked again. What started out as a list of complaints has been boiled down to tracking one marker.

Getting that marker back into range can become the main concern of the prescribing physician.

Such a patient is often too intimidated to ask why they have a low thyroid. Even if they feel a little better on the medication, they're often left with the question, "What about all my other symptoms?" The physician has treated the paper.

In my experience, this often leads to symptoms returning, sometimes with a vengeance, or new symptoms occur. If these new symptoms aren't within the speciality training of the prescribing physician, the patient is referred to someone else.

This scenario is just one example of their failure to look far enough upstream. That system leaves all kinds of healing opportunities on the table. Even worse, it can often take the real causes and true healing opportunities off the table. In this case, simple diagnosis and treatment of a specific nature is probably only going to perpetuate the cycle of trial and error.

Intelligence Gathering: The HIDDEN Causes and Dysfunctions at the Root of Most Chronic Health Complaints

We use saliva, urine, blood, and stool testing. You can also use a tissue, hair, or mineral analysis (HTMA) as it can tell something about a person that almost no other labs will reveal. It's very important which lab and lab company we use. We vetted ours over the years.

There are different ways to skin a cat. After running thousands of labs on thousands of people, I came up with the acronym H-I-D-D-E-N. We look at:

H - Hormones

I - Immune

D - Digestion

D - Detoxification

E - Energy production

N – Nervous system,

Specifically, the balance between the sympathetic and parasympathetic nervous system.

No matter what the client's problem was, those are the data points I had to have. It was mostly women who came in with any number of aches and pains, like migraines, female problems, weight, or fatigue.

The (HIDDEN) pattern took a long time to recognize. I noticed that if we worked in those (HIDDEN) areas, everyone got better.

As this investigative or *intelligence gathering* pattern was being established, we also had success in developing a holistic lifestyle program. Everyone that came into the office had five labs run, plus the online Metabolic Typing® test. (For more information, go to http://mtdiet.com).

I would explain to my prospects that we were like health detectives on a mission to look for every imbalance and healing opportunity.

"Here is what we have to look for", I'd say to them, and if they signed on, we'd order their labs and discover each person's unique healing opportunities. There was always plenty to work on in just about every person.

Important patterns were found in lifestyle changes that had to occur if the client wanted to build their health. The office I worked in was mostly for chiropractic, acupuncture, and massage. I was the nutritionist who ran the labs and, as the Health Director, I was responsible for the outcomes.

I interviewed every person walking in the door and that's how I recognized the cycle of trial and error that they were caught in. All that was great, but I started realizing it wasn't coming into the office that was helping them the most. Not as much as going home and doing the things we taught them during the period between their visits.

"You're a good patient," I would often say. "You're always showing up for your appointments, and we're tracking some progress. But it's what you do *between* visits that matters most!"

I recognized that when clients went home and slipped back into their old habits, trying to get their desired results was arduous. Often, it was when many stopped coming in. I believe they were still trapped in a certain mentality, thinking we were the ones who would fix them. I recognized, and it's especially important today, these people were still putting the control of their health in someone else's hands.

Luckily, in our office, the treatments were all drug free and required some compliance, unlike a regular doctor who would put a large percentage of patients on drugs. The same could be said for seeing a personal trainer. If you get one, if you pay the money, you're going to do exercise. If it's a nutritionist, you're going to eat better food, and so on. Many practitioners let the chips fall where they may, and the cycle of trial and error has not been broken.

Again, I realized the importance of control. The client's health needed to be in their own hands; they needed to be in control. It became a challenge trying to educate them. So, I put it all together into a step-by-step program called Functional Diagnostic Nutrition® and the DRESS for Health Success Program®.

The Components of a Holistic Lifestyle Program: DRESS for Health Success®

In this world, we all face problems. But I've also learned that we come with a certain set of instructions built into our bodies called *innate intelligence*. We all have it, it's an intelligence as obvious as gravity.

All the cells in our body know what their job is and how to do it. Built into every cell, organelle, and atom in the body is the ability and drive to be healthy. This intelligence could also be conceived as "genetic potential". If every cell is provided with everything that is genetically required to perform, and it is not overwhelmed with negative influences or interferences, it will do its job properly and health would be the natural outcome.

Our genetic potential expresses itself based on proper nourishment and other lifestyle factors, including the environment. We could call these influences "signaling".

So let us say every cell in your body knows what its job is. It's your job to provide them with good signals, like a clean environment and lifestyle. If you don't, you will pay the piper. Incidentally, I like to call the negative influences and stressors *contributors* to Metabolic Chaos®.

When we talk about the environment and this entire field of lifestyle medicine and signaling, we're really defining epigenetics. It's impossible to change your genetics or who your parents were.

You can't change the cards you were dealt with, but when it comes to epigenetic signalling, we have a lot of control. We just need to know how to individualize, how to form the right habits, and how to exercise that control.

Diet, rest, exercise, stress reduction and supplementation are super-epigenetic influences. They can provide very positive signaling to your genes, to your potential and can lead to excellent and vibrant health. By the same token, failure to eat right, go to bed on time, move our bodies appropriately, suffer stress and have a lack of specific supplementation, can provide very negative signaling. These negative signals can result in what we see today, millions of people with chronic downward-spiralling health problems.

It's imperative to provide the body with lots of nurturing. To bathe our bodies in good epigenetic influences.

Another pattern I recognized after working with thousands of people is now known worldwide. It's one of the most popular epigenetic programs. It is so successful we were granted a trademark by the US Patent and Trademark Office (USPTO). We call it DRESS for Health Success®.

D - Diet

R – Rest

E – Exercise

S - Stress reduction

S – Supplementation.

Other than seeing a physician for emergent conditions, it is really all you need to do. Anything that isn't diet, rest, exercise, or supplements falls under stress reduction. Of course, our recommendations are based on good lab data well-correlated with an individual. Stress reduction is huge and includes the environment, or the wrong foods for your Metabolic Type®.

The Role of Diet in Well-being

Your diet can be very detrimental to your well-being and can provide negative signaling. It's also a major source of stress. When you work on your diet, you're killing two birds with one stone. You're finding the right diet for you, (D), and eliminating a major source of stress (Stress reduction). Fantastic! Remember, though, there is no "one diet" that is right for everybody.

If we go back to the concept of signaling, there are some things that are good for everybody, like fresh air, sunshine, clean water. And there are some epigenetic factors that are bad for everybody, like pollution, excessive electromagnetic frequencies, some drugs, chemicals, radiation, and so on.

But when it comes to food, it's a little different. There are some food items that are bad for everyone, like too much sugar, preservatives, pesticides, chemicals, and non-food ingredients. But we are yet to identify what food is good for everybody. The first rule of thumb with food is it depends on who's eating it!

There are some foods that are right for you, and there are foods that are not. So how do we choose? It's important to remember that we all need to consume a certain ratio of protein, fat and carbohydrates. That ratio depends on the rate at which you burn your fuel (food). It is called your "oxidative rate". You may be a fast, slow, or mixed oxidizer. We call the correct fuel mixture the "macro-nutrient ratio".

Everyone has a different oxidative rate depending on their Metabolic Type®, so Metabolic Typing® and the oxidative rate become a major test for us. It is as important or even more important than A1C (hemoglobin), blood pressure, cholesterol, or dozens of other markers. By eating a macro-nutrient ratio that fuels your cells according to your genetic requirements, you are nearly approximating the diet that is bred in the bone by ancestry and genetics. This can be fine-tuned to a very satisfying level and make you feel fantastic.

Let us say 25,000 years ago (that's 500 generations ago) all your ancestors were hunter-gatherers and ate what local animals they could kill or capture. They ate a lot of meat and a lot of fat and very little carbohydrates. That's important to know as it dictates your genetic oxidative rate - the amount of protein, fat, and carbs you require. They didn't grow any grains and probably didn't eat many carbs other than seasonal fruit, berries, nuts, and edibles they could pick off the ground. That would be your correct genetic fuel mixture. I'm at my best when I eat like that, highly resistant to illness and able to maintain great physicality.

Take a different person who's say, from the mountains of South America. They ate a lot of corn and plant materials and whatever tubers they could dig up. Tribes ate over 400 varieties of potato. They ate some meat too, but once again, we see the proper fuel mixture for each person is bred in the bone from a millennium of eating a locally available diet. That's one very important feature about a person, their oxidative rate, and the proper macro nutrient ratios. If you can match that, you are going to make a huge stride forward in getting the diet that's right for you.

So, the first thing we do is to get the carb to fat, to protein ratios dialed in. Fast oxidizers may feel amazing when they consume 70% protein and fat versus only 30% carbs. Slow oxidizers may consume just 40% protein and fat and 60% carbs and be at their very best performance. The other thing to consider, and this is a little tougher, is to decide which proteins, which fats, and which carbohydrates are needed.

Because of the differences in the climate, the soils and the environment, micro-nutrient requirements differ too. For instance, where I came from 25000 years ago, the soil had certain nutrient levels, certain mineral content, certain phytonutrients. That would go into the plants, the animals would eat the plants, and then we'd eat those animals. Once again, we find nutritional requirements that are bred into the bones. Deviating from these genetic requirements can only lead to poor cellular oxidation and poor cell function.

If this sounds consuming to you, it's actually very simple to do. Believe it or not, we have a system called Metabolic Typing® at our disposal. It is better than knowing who your ancestors were, because just knowing that isn't enough. About 12,000 years ago, after the last ice age, the entire world just kind of exploded into traveling, trade, and commerce. That's when agriculture was established and spread to other things like industrialism.

The world has changed a lot during the last 25,000 years. Even if you know who your ancestors were—I have done the 23andMe gene test—you can still fail to meet your genetic requirements. It is much better today to figure it out using the Metabolic Typing® test developed by William Wolcott. This is available at http://mtdiet.com.

We also do a lot of food sensitivity testing to help a person fine-tune their diet and get off the foods they are sensitive to. Then their nourishment level goes up a notch. But food sensitivities are also a major stressor, so, again, you are getting double your money with food sensitivity testing.

How Diet, Thoughts and Emotions Can Affect Well-being

If you are not eating right, your energy will go down and so will your satiation. Satiety is critical to avoid cravings and over-indulgence. It is not fun to be unsatisfied with your meals. There are key indicators for what your satiation is. You can grade the amount of energy you get from food and grade your sense of well-being too. It's easy when you know how.

And wow, what else do you want from a meal besides satiation, good energy, and a sense of well-being? Running labs and figuring out all the upstream areas that need improvement are important. But nothing has a greater influence epigenetically than getting the diet right for one's type.

I can't tell you how many people's lives were improved just by changing breakfast! For some people, it's a complete turnaround.

"I can't believe that two hours later, I am still not hungry. I have no cravings; I feel fully satisfied and I feel pretty happy." This is the typical comment we get.

If you're walking around grumpy for no reason, you're not satisfied, and you're craving things, then you're not eating the right food and macro-nutrient ratios. That's your body telling you the previous meal was not right for you. Most likely, the protein, fat, and carb ratios were off. It's easy to dial it in using the Diet Check Record sheet (DCRs) included with the Metabolic Typing® test at https://mtdiet.com/ Remember, it's not just diet. You need to be well-rested, hydrated, and you need to exercise. Supplements can also be very helpful.

Then there is stress. Mental or emotional stress from work, relationships, or financial concerns, etc., can put you in a bad mood or make your head spin. We found some people were eating right, going to bed on time, and exercising, yet they still had problems. Sometimes those problems were found in the complexities within the mind and emotions.

The DRESS program still applies here because everything that is not Diet, Rest, Exercise, or Supplements can increase stress, especially the hidden stressors like a racing mind. Sometimes stress is resolved by simply changing your body chemistry through correcting your diet, taking supplements, and so on. There is also training on how to meditate and separate oneself from a racing mind. It starts with realizing that you are not your mind and you are not your emotions, just like you are not your body, either.

Let's say your body is an accumulation of the food you've eaten throughout your life. True. If you lost your arms or legs, would you still be there? Yes. The same is true of thoughts and emotions. You can separate from them, and you will still be there. Negative thoughts, emotions, and impressions accumulate throughout your life, and much of it is just a bunch of junk. They are not you. You are not your thoughts, or your emotions, or your body.

Recommendations for People Who are Dealing with Chronic Disease

Let's talk about dealing with chronic downward-spiraling disease processes. I want to emphasize that people need to take charge of their own health. I strongly suggest that miracle-like results can, and do, occur when we work on correcting imbalances and restoring resiliency.

I had a client with a classic case of chronic stress-related complaints. Her lifestyle needed a major tune up. She was overweight, tired, and fatigued. She suffered frequent headaches, had foggy thinking, aches and pains, alternating constipation and loose stools and general malaise. With the support of her husband, they decided they wanted to hire a health coach. We didn't use that term back then, but we started working together right away. This was long ago before I coined all my phrases and before I founded Functional Diagnostic Nutrition®.

She ran all my HIDDEN labs - hormone, immune, digestion, detoxification, energy production, and nervous system balancing, and we got her started on a DRESS for Health Success® program. I was practicing what is now considered standard FDN. It's the same program I did for my mother! It's what I do for everybody, and it is what thousands of practitioners do after completing my training program.

A few months later, my phone rang, and it was this client. I thought something must be wrong.

"Reed, I just had to call and tell you how happy "Scott and I are!" she said, sounding like she was about to cry. "We just left the doctor's office and… we're pregnant!"

"Congratulations!" I said, relieved, but slightly mystified. She had never indicated she was trying to get pregnant.

"No, you don't understand. Scott and I gave up trying to have a baby nine years ago, so we never mentioned it. But when we left the doctor's office a few minutes ago, we both looked at each other and said, 'REED'! You're the one who helped me get healthy enough to have a baby and so we just wanted to thank you!"

I felt like I'd just hit a hole-in-one on the golf course. Now that would be a real miracle. Since then, that same story has been repeated many times in the history of FDN. When you get healthy enough, when you restore balance and resiliency, it can feel like a miracle has occurred.

If you are caught in the cycle of trial and error, if you have a complaint that bothers you often and it has been going on for a long time–and you want to fix it, then perhaps FDN is worth looking into. It's easy to do. Functional laboratory tests are simple to complete. The kits get shipped to your home or place of business so we can investigate all 6 areas of concern. You'll get clear instructions on how to take your tests and send them to the labs. During this time, you can also fill out some intake forms so we can learn everything about you.

You can meet with an FDN® Practitioner to get acquainted and discuss your health history and health goals. It takes about 2 weeks for your lab results to be processed, and when all the data is in, you meet with your FDN® again for your "Results and Recommendations" session.

Multiple sessions are usually required to learn how to apply our signature DRESS for Health Success® protocol. We cannot make any guarantees because we do not control the outcomes. But what we can tell you is that by the end of six sessions, most clients feel good again and have achieved significant results.

CHAPTER 2

Breath

By Pantea Kalhor, Publisher, Four Times Best-selling Author, Certified Fertility and PTSD Coach

Since childhood, I spent most days of the week at the hospital, not as a patient but as a daughter of a head nurse supervisor. I saw a lot of blood, pain, surgeries, and people who were anxiously waiting to see a doctor. My mom had to take care of the whole hospital, so every time I had to look for her, I would have to go from one ward to another.

One day, while she was working in the women's ward, I saw a box. It did not seem like a medicine box or anything else I was used to. There was no label on it, so I asked the secretary what it was.

"That's a dead infant," she said. "She didn't make it and so I have to make arrangements for legal paperwork."

As an 8–year-old, I wondered how the secretary could be so calm talking about and looking at the dead infant. I also realized there must have been a lot of heart-breaking moments behind that unmarked box. Nine months of hope and waiting for the birth, then a lot of wasted time, all hidden inside.

My mom took me to the labor room once, so I understood a little of what goes on. I could hear painful screams coming from mothers who were delivering a new life into the world. I saw blood and smelled the antiseptic and medical equipment. It was a lot for an 8-year-old to process.

I remember how my mom worked tirelessly and sometimes had to stay in for the night shift. Our house was lifeless without mom, and I didn't like it. Every day, she talked to my dad during lunch and dinner about all the cases she saw in the hospital. Mostly about the complicated, negative, or acute cases.

My poor dad had to listen and respond to her during his meal. I didn't like that either. So, I promised myself, I would have a clean job with no blood, surgery, night shifts, acute cases, or dead baby boxes.

My mom would have loved me to be a doctor. It was the reason she showed me the reality of working in the hospital environment. I remember being 17 years old and having to make the choice about what career path I would take. The university entry exam was approaching fast, and with all the presumption, I thought maybe my mother was right. Maybe I should pursue medicine.

Until one day, just another normal day, I went to the hospital after school to walk home with mom. Walking home with her was fun. We'd talk about my day at school, my friends, and on the way sometimes, we went to the market and did some shopping.

But on this day, I found her with a bunch of medical students all in their white uniforms. She was explaining their responsibilities in their new ward. As I was standing there watching, an overwhelming fear flooded over me and settled on my chest. All the previous overwhelming experiences of blood, pain, screams, loss, and the dead box would not let it budge. My future, the future my mom wanted me to have, was the last thing I wanted.

Escaping is all I could think about. I had to escape, and I needed fresh air. I ran out of the hospital as fast as I could and caught a taxi home. By the end of the day, I had decided to become a software engineer. A classic job which only needed my brain and intelligence. I imagined myself in an office dressed formally with high heels on, sitting in front of a computer, coding, programming, and solving problems. Now, my future looked bright and promising. I knew everyone needed computers, and every industry would be computerized. Looking back, I see destiny had another plan for me.

Where Did My Health Journey Start?

Software engineering opened so many doors for personal development. I found my way to Australia to continue my education and obtain my master's degree in information technology. In 2005, while studying in my second year of university, I yearned for an adventure. Australia is a beautiful country with incredible scenery. It's the perfect place for surfing, diving, and snorkeling in their blue oceans: the Southern, Pacific, and Indian Ocean, as well as the Timor, Tasman, and Coral Seas.

I'd always dreamed of diving and snorkeling in the Great Barrier Reef in Queensland, with colorful Angelfish, Butterfly Fish, Cardinal Fish, Damselfish, Gobies, Groupers. I excluded swimming with sharks from that list. So, I decided it was time to start diving classes. We trained in a swimming pool in Canberra where I lived. It sounded fun and easy.

The training was tough. Carrying heavy oxygen tanks on my back was grueling, especially on a tiny 45-kg body like mine. We trained for a few days in the pool for a dive to the depth of 18-meters in open water. Then we went to Batemans Bay, the closest beach to Canberra. We drove along the shoreline of the South Pacific Ocean, the far southern reaches of the Sydney Basin, a 148 km drive from Canberra.

I had over 10 teammates. I met new, adventurous people, a female police officer, young university students, a man in his 60s who was also bringing his dream into reality. There was a father and his daughter who loved to spend quality time together. Apart from the training, I had a great time getting to know these people, dining, chatting, laughing, and learning with them.

The first dive was the worst. The instructors told us to dive to an 18-meter depth and practice what we'd learned in the swimming pool. We'd practiced how to sit or stand down there, how to communicate what we needed with body language, and how to put our mask back on if it was accidentally removed. Also, how to help someone if they ran out of oxygen by sharing our own masks all without gulping in any water.

We were told not to touch anything underwater and if we saw sharks, to stay calm and not allow them to feel our fears. I'd done well with all these exercises in the swimming pool, and I thought I knew them all. But reality was soon to make itself known.

We hopped on the boat and didn't stop until the depth-sounder measured 18 metres depth. One by one, we flipped backwards into the water with our tanks on, holding onto our masks. As I descended, I equalized the air pressure by holding my nose to protect my ears. We all swam to the bottom. I showed my instructor how I could balance by standing and sitting on the sand below.

After practicing a few steps, the instructor took off my mask and asked me to put it back on. That was the scariest experience of my life so far. I suddenly panicked and forgot all about the training. There was no way out. I was under the weight of 18-metres of water, and it was too high to reach without air, without my mask.

"That's it," I thought. "I'm not going to make it."

All the team watched anxiously and tried to talk to me in body language.

"I want to live," I remember thinking. "I still have a lot of life ahead; for God's sake, I was not even 30."

Sheer will kicked in and I collected myself. My training came back to me, and I put the mask up against my face and exhaled what little air I had left in my lungs. It didn't work. As I inhaled, I gulped a lot of salty water, but I had no choice. I tried again and again until finally the water drained out of the mask, and I could breathe oxygen.

I immediately looked up. The sun beams penetrated the water and shone down towards me. But at 18 meters I couldn't see the sun itself. I knew it should be shining, and there was a big blue sky and seagulls awaiting me. All I could think about was getting out. I pushed off from the bottom and kicked as hard as I could, but it seemed like it would take forever to get to the surface. Never had I experienced such intense hunger for a deep breath of fresh air. I kept telling myself that I was still alive, and I could make it.

That was the worst and best day of my life. Worst, because I experienced how close death can bc, and the best because I knew how to survive.

I couldn't have imagined how much that event could affect the rest of my life. A few months after the incident, I couldn't sleep from the pain I felt when I coughed, and shortness of breath. I'd never had asthma. As a child I had a few allergies, and I caught a cold easily. But I'd never had shortness of breath like this.

I visited the doctor at the university, and he diagnosed me with asthma. That was the first time I used an inhaler. Over the next few years, my breath slowly improved, but then I immigrated to Canada. The cold Canadian winter exacerbated my respiratory condition.

I went from one doctor to another and tried numerous types of inhalers. I'd be fine for a year or a few months until the beginning of winter, then asthma would come back again.

I got married in October 2013, and we had real difficulty trying to get pregnant. I had one treatment after another, and nothing seemed to work. After paying hefty prices for in vitro fertilization (IVF) treatments, IUI (a type of artificial insemination), and fertility medication, we gave up.

Then, I had acupuncture and looked into holistic medicine. I got familiar with the world of possibilities, and it gave me hope. Surprisingly, my asthma was one of the issues that needed to be addressed for my fertility treatment. I cut out eating dairy products and any food that caused inflammation. I replaced my diet with only organic and whole foods.

Looking back, I still admire the power of traditional Chinese medicine in finding healing opportunities and looking at the body as a whole system. While I compared my functional lab results with the acupuncture diagnosis, I could see the similarities in their analysis.

My acupuncturist addressed my asthma, inflammation, and liver congestion[1] as blockers for my fertility issues. Now, after years, I could still see liver congestion and estrogen dominancy in my functional test results. Liver filters the blood and regulates chemical levels. If the liver can't function properly, it can't remove extra estrogen that has built up over time and the level of estrogen goes high in our body; we call this estrogen dominancy. That means our estrogen level is relatively higher than progesterone and that is one of the reason women have fertility issues[2]. In chapter 4, Dr. Tara

---

[1] Liver (Anatomy): Picture, Function, Conditions, Tests, Treatments,

https://www.webmd.com/digestive-disorders/picture-of-the-liver

[2]Signs and Symptoms of High Estrogen,

https://www.healthline.com/health/high-estrogen

Scott talks in more details about estrogen dominancy and resolving fertility issues.

I included gentle exercise, and we enjoyed a more joyful and relaxing lifestyle. I had acupuncture treatments regularly, and finally, we conceived our baby girl, naturally. Blessed with the great joy of motherhood, I started researching and interviewing holistic and integrative medicine practitioners and created "Pantea Kalhor Transition Channel" on YouTube[3] and podcast platforms. The more I interviewed experts, the more I wanted to learn. I started fertility coaching, but I knew something was still missing.

Then the pandemic hit, and I had to take care of my baby at home. As a result, I became isolated from the outside world. I couldn't swim regularly, and I felt my health deteriorate. Then my asthma came back.

The turning point came when I was lucky enough to interview Reed Davis, the founder of Functional Nutrition Diagnostic certification course. I became familiar with the concept, and I wanted to fill the gap in my health issues and then help my fertility clients.

I found the missing piece of the puzzle and studied it in depth so I could become a Functional Medical Practitioner and incorporate it

---

[3] https://www.youtube.com/c/PanteaKalhorTransitionChannel

into my fertility coaching. I ordered functional medicine labs for myself to find out the root cause of my asthma.

Functional medicine practitioners usually run a few fundamental labs to find healing opportunities through investigating:

- Hormone levels: Cortisol, Estrogen, Progesterone, or sex hormones
- Gut, liver, and small intestinal functions
- Protein digestion
- Autoimmunity system

I was surprised to find out how low my cortisol level was and how exhausted my body felt to stay in balance. I had some gut issues without knowing it; high total Bile Acids (in urine test) which could indicate liver issues and low melatonin[4] that explained shortage of sleep. These weren't often caught in conventional lab testing and some medical doctors didn't even see the need to look for hidden layers.

The range of results is narrower in functional medicine labs. If you did the same labs in a regular laboratory, they may look normal because the range is too wide to catch the problem. Once, I remember I asked my family doctor to run a cortisol test for me and

---

[4] Melatonin: What You Need to Know,
Melatonin: What You Need To Know | NCCIH (nih.gov)

he dismissed me with a laugh, then avoided me. "We don't normally do this type of test for someone in your case," he said.

Medical doctors who are open to learn about holistic medicine, and believe in mind-body connection modalities, always consider treating the body as a whole. They don't rely on one diagnosis because of specific symptoms and believe that even childhood and past traumas can count as hidden stressors that impact our health. They are not trying to just treat the lab results or remove the symptoms. If the hidden root cause can't be caught in the body, the symptoms will be back on the surface again. That's the reason why cancer survivors are always on the edge of meeting their cancer again.

As a certified fertility and PTSD (Post Traumatic Stress Disorder) coach and podcaster, I've interviewed over 175 episodes with top experts in PTSD, fertility, and holistic medicine. I've learned that many chronic diseases originate from fear, emotional discomfort, trauma, and mental issues.

Unfortunately, many cancer patients and other chronic disease warriors only visit doctors when the symptoms are unbearable, or uncomfortable to live with. Their body and hormone levels are on a roller coaster trying to adjust and fight all the time until they get too exhausted to adjust. Problematic issues can accumulate on the cellular level and cause a lot of discomfort, especially long term.

The body has a great mechanism to fight, balance hormones, and secretes enzymes to help it get back to normal again. But by the time our vital reserves diminish in a way the body cannot cope with, it's usually too late to compensate.

I also discovered not every diet type is appropriate for each person depending how our digestion system, allergies, and our overall health look. We should all have a customized diet plan contingent on how severely our health has deteriorated. Getting it back to normal may vary with time. For some, it's shorter than others depending on how severe their health crisis is.

Looking back to my teenage years, I appreciate the hard work medical doctors and health practitioners did to protect their patients, remembering days I spent in the hospital with my mom. Saving lives and optimizing other people's health are great missions that I am also interested in learning more in-depth day by day.

My friend complained about having itchy skin.

"The doctor gave me a pomade," she said. "Whenever I use it, I feel great, but then the itching starts again a few days later."

Is this story familiar to you? This is a very common story for so many.

"Have you ever tried to find the root cause of your issue?" I asked. "Maybe you have some other hidden imbalances you're not aware of." She just stared at me.

"How should I know?"

It reminded me how much we are all responsible for the health of our body and mind. If you suffer from a long-term disease and have tried numerous treatments and medications to no avail, I recommend looking for a complementary medicine provider.

A Few Recommendations for Optimal Health

Here are a few small adjustments you can follow to improve your health:

- Find a functional medicine practitioner and run thorough functional labs to find the healing opportunities in your body.
- Practice breathwork. You can refer to chapter three and learn how right breath can extend longevity.
- Have a relaxing day with your family or friends at least once per week apart from your work or daily tasks.

Help yourself daily by:

- Get sufficient amounts of sleep.
- Choose a customized diet plan.

- Create a regular exercise plan.
- Relax.
- Meditate.
- Stop rushing and multitasking.

Take the time to enjoy your meal:

- Smell it.
- Enjoy the garnishing and colors.
- Chew slowly and enjoy the taste of every bite.
- Listen to relaxing music.

Lastly, never lose hope. Be proactive and create a clear vision for your health and recovery.

CHAPTER 3

A Secret to Longevity: Breathwork

By Dr. Defne Nayman, MD, Anti-Aging, Functional, & Metabolic Medicine

In New York City, over ten years ago, I remember being in the middle of a very busy Emergency Room looking at loads of patients layered in cabbage style. I knew in my heart that some of them did not need to be there. They wouldn't be there if they had been provided with the right tools to take care of their health.

I wouldn't be pronouncing 50–60-year-old patients dead and giving the worst possible news to their loved ones. Witnessing the lifestyle outcomes in the ER (Emergency Room) was challenging in many ways, including personally. These experiences prompted me to seek other ways to help people; not just to prevent illnesses, but to guide them to live their lives to their fullest potential.

I remember a special moment when I was running along the East Side highway; I was ruminating about the night before when I resuscitated a young man who ended up in the ICU brain-dead. That is when it hit me! I recall making a pledge to myself that I would serve beyond providing resuscitation.

Driven by my quest, I discovered Anti-Aging/Functional and Metabolic Medicine. I immediately realized this new world of medicine was going to shape the future. Following through with the training, I started assessing my health battles. Conventional medicine doesn't provide you with the tools to take care of yourself the right way and I wasn't in a good state physically or mentally.

I was blessed with a family. My son was my priority. In fact, he was in the spotlight of my life. My family, my friends, everybody else came before me. So, even though I had the tools, it wasn't necessarily easy for me to start taking care of myself. At my lowest point, I had gained over 30 pounds. I looked wasted as my stress hormones bottomed out and my thyroid took a hit. I decided it was time to apply the knowledge and the tools.

When you are guided with the right tools and take ownership of your own health, there are limitless possibilities. I feel and look much younger than I did five to ten years ago. In fact, I have the exercise capacity of my 30s. I lost about 30 pounds and I was able to achieve all of this by applying simple, wholesome lifestyle measures and making my health a priority.

Mind-body healing, nutrition, detoxification, hormonal balancing, and reversal of rapid aging are the pillars of the process.

With years of experience in medicine, I recognized that the mind and body connection is at the center of many processes of healing. Recently, this awareness inspired me to study breathwork. Realizing that I was a poor breather, breathwork became a personal interest as well. I am humbled by the opportunity to share my knowledge with you. Breathwork helps create a state of healing and regeneration.

My Introduction to Breathwork

The very first time I learned about breathwork was at an online functional medicine conference. It had a wide-reaching attendance and Sachin Patel, a provider, and mentor, guided us through an amazing breathwork experience that lasted about 60 minutes. I didn't know what to expect.

We started by shaking off our bodies to fast-paced music. Then we were guided through a sequence of breathing techniques. Following our breathwork, we eased into a peaceful meditation where we had a conversation with our younger selves. I remember having an intense release of emotions and crying. I learned breathwork allows you to tap into this emotional state, which subsequently facilitates getting into the meditative as well as the grateful zone. By the end of the session, I'd had an incredible breakthrough and was left with some intense emotions.

When you own your breath, nobody can steal your peace.

What Is Breathwork?

Breathwork is an intentional practice to alter our breathing through different sets of exercises. These exercises help us achieve physical, spiritual, and mental well-being.

As part of breathwork, one needs to understand the dynamics and distinguish between good and bad breathing. It involves learning how to optimize breathing in ways that would be most beneficial.

The average human takes about 20,000 - 25,000 breaths per day. Our breathing quality is incredibly influential on our health. Each breath makes us healthier or creates more problems.

The Effects of Poor Breathing

- Alters the gasses (oxygen, carbon dioxide, nitric oxide) that are essential for optimal health.
- Limits the body's ability to utilize oxygen and shifts the PH (acidity) of the blood.
- Optimal energy is not created.
- Nervous System stays on high alert all the time—improper breathing sends the wrong signals.
- Cardiovascular system is overworked—faster breathing increases heart rate and blood pressure.
- Poor Circulation ensues due to constriction of the blood vessels (with low CO2).

- Sleep quality is altered—snoring, apnea, frequent urination.
- Facial structure changes—mouth breathing affects teeth and face structure, especially in adolescents.
- Airways become restricted—mouth breathing can cause nasal and other airways to atrophy or weaken.
- Poor lung function—shallow breathing can lead to inefficient lung function and over time, lung damage.
- Suboptimal protein performance follows due to changes in PH, involving enzymes, antibodies, hemoglobin, …
- Increased stress and inflammation dumps adrenaline to widen airways, which also leads to inflammation of the airways. Then cortisol is released to reduce inflammation. A vicious cycle can create a chronic situation.

Correcting and improving our breathing will improve these issues.

In a nutshell, the idea is to "utilize breath for health". This concept has been used in Eastern medicine for thousands of years. In India it's called Pranayama, "control of life force". In the west now, there is a growing body of research as modern medicine is catching up on the benefits.

There is an article from Harvard Medical University documenting the relationship between breathwork and stress reduction.[5]

Also, a study was published in the "Journal in Neurophysiology" demonstrating the link between breath and brain activity

Breathwork Ensures Optimal:

- Oxygenation in the lungs.
- Oxygen delivery and exchange at tissue level.
- Carbon dioxide and nitric oxide levels.
- Blood PH (acidity) levels.

The benefits are profound:

1. One exceptionally powerful benefit is that we tap into our nervous system, and we regulate our parasympathetic and sympathetic nervous responses.

2. We can easily tap into our emotional state and regulate our feelings of anxiety, depression, and other mood issues, including PTSD.

[5] Relaxation techniques: Breath control helps quell errant stress response,

https://www.health.harvard.edu/mind-and-mood/relaxation-techniques-breath-control-helps-quell-errant-stress-response

With the breathwork, most of the clients experience better outlook in life, calmness, and happiness; so, it can work like an anti-depressant, especially when used long term[6]. [7]

3. Breathwork enables people to focus, increase their awareness, and enrich their creativity.
4. After each session, one can experience more clarity.
5. Sessions help access a deeper sleep which is restorative.
6. Our immune system works more efficiently.
7. Breathwork helps reduce inflammation in our body.
8. We can achieve enhanced athletic performance.

So, on so forth.

Breathwork vs Yoga and Meditation

Although breathwork and meditation can achieve results that overlap, there are differences. I have been working with people who teach yoga and meditation. They all confirm that breathwork is a completely different approach.

---

[6]How Breath-Control Can Change Your Life, https://www.ncbi.nlm.nih.gov/pmc/articles/PMC6137615/

[7]Nasal Respiration Entrains Human Limbic Oscillations and Modulates Cognitive Function,
https://www.jneurosci.org/content/36/49/12448

During breathwork, we simply practice various techniques to regulate our breathing. With meditation or yoga, we observe how we breathe, practice deep breathing, and create awareness.

With breathwork, we purposefully alter our breathing, and we have access to a wide variety of breathing techniques which achieve different states, including energizing our body, increasing focus, and more. Breathwork is simple if you follow the breathing techniques. As meditation can be challenging for some, with breathwork, there is no need to stress about getting into a meditative state.

How Breathwork Can Help Asthma

Once the basic elements of optimal breathing are properly attained, it makes a substantial improvement in asthma symptoms. The nostrils humidify and clean the inhaled air and stimulate the lungs for better air exchange.

Nitric oxide, which helps oxygenation at the cellular level, is a product of our sinuses. Nose breathing allows us to carry this gas all the way down into our lungs. A significant number of people are mouth breathers, especially at night-time, so mouth taping is highly recommended.

Mouth taping forces us to breathe through our noses, which makes a substantial impact on our health. Mouth breathers experience lower energy, poor lung functions, suboptimal oxygenation, increased stress, inflammation, and so on. If you consider mouth taping, start 15-20 minutes before going to bed to see how it feels. Some people feel very uncomfortable in the beginning, however, once you get used to it, and you're able to sleep with it, you will rise and shine well-rested, and in a much better mood.

When we talk about taking a deep breath, the emphasis is made on the inhalation (breathing the air in). However, it's more about the exhalation (breathing the air out). Focusing on taking the time to exhale is vitally important. Optimal breathing calls for longer exhalation (see below). "Take a big deep breath" also suggests taking a large volume of breath in. It is about the depth of the breath, not the volume.

Another essential principle of breathing is to use our diaphragm while breathing; this is called diaphragmatic breathing, or abdominal breathing. Here is where the depth comes into play. Most view breathing with "puffed out chest and tucked in belly" as attractive since it makes one look slimmer. Yet it is recommended that we engage our diaphragm about 70 to 80 percent of each breath.

Abdominal Breathing Has Multiple Benefits:

1. We are basically using our diaphragm as a pistol. Besides ventilation, this pistol function also aids in detoxification by pulling lymphatic fluid from the internal organs, such as the

liver and intestinal system. The diaphragm is the most important muscle for an athlete. The foundation of athletic endurance, performance, and strength rests upon a strong diaphragm. Breathing with our diaphragm and practicing this throughout the day is very beneficial.

2. It increases blood and oxygen supply to cells.

In addition to the basics of breathing, good posture is imperative as it assists in optimal air entry and oxygen exchange.

Practical Exercise for Optimal Breathing Sessions

Optimal Breath is about inhaling for 1-3-seconds, exhaling for 3-5-seconds with a 1-3-second pause. You can pick the timing that works for you so long as the inhale is shorter than the exhale, and there is a pause before you repeat. Keep in mind that abdominal breathing is part of this exercise. Practicing this breath throughout the day is also going to create muscle memory to help regulate your breathing.

Optimal breathing is about 8 to 12 breaths per minute. Breathing faster only works up our cardiovascular system and our nervous system. We want to breathe slowly, and we also want to avoid breathing in high volumes. When I first started with breathwork, I was taking rather big breaths and feeling dizzy. I later realized that it is not the volume, it’s the depth that matters.

Breathwork exercises, other than "optimal breath", vary in intensity, speed, etc. These exercises are used to build resilience in our body and to control breathing. It's not something you should do continually.

Balance Breathing

Balance breathing is the ideal breathwork, the ultimate goal, but it takes a considerable amount of time and practice to achieve. Yogis are the experts. They also call it the 5.5-second breath; inhaling for 5.5 seconds and exhaling in 5.5-seconds. Balance breathing is a goal to aspire to once you've achieved an advanced level of breathwork.

Alternate Nostril Breathing

Alternate nose breathing is a method used to get into a balanced physiological state. Did you know that throughout the day, our nostrils take turns, so we don't breathe from both at the same time? Every couple of hours, one gets engorged to block the passage while the other one stays open. It's the bodies' way to regulate our physiology.

The right side is the "masculine" side or the "sympathetic" side. If we breathe through our right nostril, we're stimulated and energized. If we breathe through our left nostril, it triggers the right side of the brain, and we activate the "parasympathetic" relaxed state. Alternate nostril breathing calms us down and helps us find balance.

Start inhaling with the left nostril. Close your right nostril and inhale for 3-seconds. Then close the left nostril, open the right, and exhale for 6-seconds. Inhale on that same side for 3-seconds, then alternate. Use this technique for a few minutes to achieve balance.

Yogic Coffee

One of my favorite breathing exercises is yogic coffee. It's a great pick-me-up to boost your energy when you don't want to drink coffee. This technique is all about breathing at a rapid pace in and out through your nose.

Sit up straight and have your arms hanging at your side. Coordinate your breathing with your hands. Breathe in and lift your hands up into the air, then exhale as your hands come down and make fists. Breathe this way for 10 to 20 sets, take a break for a few breaths, then repeat for another 2-sets.

Box Breathing

Box breathing is a method commonly used to bring tranquility and peace. This technique allows you to choose how many seconds you want to count. Your options are three, four, or five seconds. The box stands for inhalation, pause, and exhalation. Some also add a pause after exhalation. I prefer to count for 4-seconds.

For example, take a breath in for 4-seconds, hold it for 4-seconds, and then exhale for 4-seconds. Add the optional 4-second hold after you've exhaled if you prefer. You can do box breathing for a few rounds as an efficient way to calm down if you feel stressed or upset.

Buzz breath

Buzz breathing is the practice of humming as we exhale through our nose with a closed mouth. Our bodies have different gases in play when it comes to breathwork:

- Oxygen - A necessity.
- Carbon dioxide - Considered a villain, but it turns out to be the most important gas in terms of regulating our breathing.
- Nitric oxide - Produced in our sinuses and in the lining of our blood vessels.

When we practice buzz breathing, nitric oxide is produced in our sinuses up to 15x more. As we breathe in, we inhale the nitric oxide all the way down into our lungs, which then dilates the vessels and improves the oxygen-carbon dioxide exchange.

First, take a big, deep breath in through your nose and hold it for 15 seconds. Then, as you exhale steadily through your nose, hum. Immediately after exhaling completely, take another couple of deep breaths. This way, you'll be able to carry the nitric oxide right down into your lungs for the gas exchange.

Studies have shown the benefits of buzz breathing to be substantial in both increasing blood flow and lowering blood pressure.

4-7-8 Breathing Exercise

This one is great for rapid relaxation to ease your body into sleep. Inhale through your nose for 4-seconds, hold for 7-seconds, then exhale through your nose for 8-seconds.

How To Unblock Your Nose

This technique is for people who have nasal congestion and can easily replace medications. Remember, our nose gets congested physiologically to block the air entry for balance.

Breathe normally for a few times, then at the end of an exhale, pinch your nose and nod your head back and forth until you have the urge to breathe. You want that urge to get more intense until you cannot hold it any longer. Breathe normally again and repeat for a few rounds.

Many people have experienced a significant reduction in congestion with this exercise. Nasal mucosal engorgement and congestion are used physiologically all day long, so this exercise enables you to use it to your advantage.

A Secret to Longevity

"The secret to longevity is to keep breathing."

Sophie Tucker

I love this statement because it resonates with my practice. Leticia's quote is powerful too, as it reminds us that breathing is a way to achieve spiritual healing.

"Inhale the future, exhale the past."

Leticia Rae

The breath is the link between the mind and the body, and a powerful tool to regulate our bodies. Is your breath making you sick or is it making you healthy?

If you are new to this concept, I recommend you start by working on optimizing your breath. Whenever you find yourself breathing from your mouth, close it and intently breathe from your nose. It's crucial to focus on your breathing, incorporate your diaphragm and fix your posture as it substantiates the effects of every breath.

These breathing exercises can be done any time of the day, and once you practice optimal breathing daily, you teach your brain how to breathe better. With every passing day, you'll enable your body to function in the most favorable way by tapping into your mind, body, and spirit connection.

A recommended reference: *Breath* by James Nestor

CHAPTER 4

Hidden Causes of Infertility

By Dr. Tara Scott, MD, Gynecologist, Functional Medicine Practitioner

I am a traditionally trained Medical Doctor. I started my career in OB-GYN (Obstetrics Gynecology); Once I finished my training, I joined a private practice, where I was very busy delivering babies and performing surgeries.

When it came time for me to get pregnant, I had some difficulty. I'd always had painful periods and suspected I could have endometriosis. I took an oral medication called Clomid, also known as clomiphene citrate. It's used to treat female infertility. Luckily, the first time I took Clomid, I conceived my first child.

The second time around, I had trouble getting pregnant again. I had 6-cycles of Clomid and saw infertility specialists. I went through all the workups, had a laparoscopic surgery which confirmed that I did in fact have endometriosis. They prescribed more fertility medications.

After 11 failed cycles, I got pregnant but suffered a miscarriage. It was heart-breaking. But once again, I took more fertility medications, until I finally did In Vitro Fertilization (IVF). I was blessed with twins but had a complicated pregnancy. I was on bed rest for 14 weeks, which ended with a complicated delivery. Nevertheless, I now have three wonderful children.

These experiences led to an interest in female hormones, which I studied until I became a certified menopause practitioner.

Then 14 years ago, my brother suddenly passed away. He was only 38. He had a heart attack while he was hiking, and although he had a lot of risk factors, including diabetes, I believe it was a preventable death.

This was enough motivation to focus even more on wellness and prevention in women's health and hormones. I learned that if you have estrogen dominance, or any issues that puts you at risk of diabetes, you could also be susceptible to cancer in the uterus and breasts.

I now hold a board certification in Functional Medicine, Integrative Medicine and OB-GYN. The majority of my patients have women's health and hormone disorders. I also treat patients who are trying to get pregnant but need help to correct their imbalances to optimize their fertility.

My Story and What I Would Do Differently

I learned I had a problem with estrogen detoxification. Our bodies have a genetic process that involves methylation. Methylation is just one of the enzymatic processes that is used when your body detoxes or tries to clear used estrogen.

I had a genomic evaluation, so I could see which enzymes weren't working correctly. I have MTHFR (methylene-TetraHydroFolate reductase). It's an enzyme in the body that plays a vital role and a genetic mutation that can lead to high levels of homocysteine in the blood and low levels of folate and other vitamins[8].

Other adjustments put me at risk for miscarriage and inhibited my body's ability to get rid of estrogen. Another contributing factor to my infertility was Hashimoto's thyroiditis (an increased risk of miscarriage and subfertility). At that time, I was just offered medications. They never looked any further. They never bothered to find the root cause.

After learning that gluten intolerance is linked to Hashimoto's, I eliminated that out of my diet, and my thyroid antibodies improved. I also concentrated on my gut health and dealt with bacteria that can

[8] MTHFR Gene Variants: Symptoms, Treatment, Testing, and More,

http://www.healthline.com/health/mthfr-gene

be associated with autoimmune issues. Furthermore, I balanced my own hormones and worked on my estrogen detox. I still ended up having a second surgery for endometriosis, but when I had my third for a tubal ligation, there was no sign of endometriosis at all.

I had healed my endometriosis and have pictures from my surgeries to prove it. Balancing my hormones, reversing my Hashimoto's, maximizing my estrogen detox, and working at the cellular level was successful for me; although not everyone may have the same result.

Can Women with Hashimoto's Still Get Pregnant?

Hashimoto's thyroiditis is an autoimmune condition where your cells attack your thyroid. There is a high correlation with gluten intolerance and dietary imbalances. However, sometimes it is not gluten or dairy. When your thyroid antibodies are high, it correlates with the severity of symptoms.

When I see patients with Hashimoto's, the first thing I do is put them on an anti-inflammatory diet. We recommend they go both dairy-free and gluten-free. But for some patients, we slow the process down and only eliminate one at a time.

Often, we will do a stool test that looks for a PCR (Polymerase Chain Reaction) of the bacteria in your gut, or your microbiome. It tests to see if there are any abnormalities in the microbiome. Then we address that as well. Some studies in mainstream literature say treating thyroid with thyroid medication will help prevent the progression of Hashimoto's thyroiditis, especially in the guise of infertility, and early pregnancy.

I am not opposed to treating with thyroid medications when it is indicated. But most practitioners only monitor the TSH (Thyroid-Stimulating Hormone) levels to see if the thyroid is making enough hormones. They don't look at the free triiodothyronine (T3), or the thyroxine free (T4) tests, or check the antibodies[9].

We have a much better outcome with our patients and their symptom management when we assess all tests (TSH, T3, T4 and monitoring antibodies)[10].

Reverse T3 is another thyroid test we recommend. However, even in the Reverse T3, we can't always find the right ratios of thyroid hormones. Some people prefer to go to a purer form, or they might need to have a compounded thyroid medication. Others may need a combination of T3 and T4, which is not common in traditional medicine. Getting their thyroid function exactly right has been helpful in optimizing not only their health but also their fertility.

---

[9] What are T3, T4, and TSH?
https://www.endocrineweb.com/thyroid-what-are-t3-t4-tsh

[10] What Is Reverse T3?
https://www.endocrineweb.com/conditions/thyroid/what-reverse-t3

What Is PCOS, And How Is It Treated?

Polycystic Ovarian Syndrome (PCOS) is a hormone disorder found mainly in women of reproductive age. Clinical diagnosis can show high androgens (male hormones), which are testosterone and DHEA (Dehydroepiandrosterone).

PCOS is commonly diagnosed by Rotterdam criteria [11] .

- Oligo-ovulation or anovulation: (Anovulation happens when an egg (ovum) doesn't release from your ovary during your menstrual cycle and results in irregular periods
- Hyperandrogenism: Excessive presence of the male sex hormones testosterone[12].
- Clinical (including signs such as hirsutism) or biological (including a raised free androgen index or free testosterone).
- Polycystic ovaries visible on ultrasound: indicating a polycystic appearance of ovaries or a volume of over 10 centimeters.

Even aforesaid criteria are not necessarily reasons for diagnosis.

---

[11]The Rotterdam Criteria for Diagnosing PCOS - PERLA Health, https://perlahealth.com/the-rotterdam-criteria-for-diagnosing-pcos/

[12]Hyperandrogenism, https://www.topdoctors.co.uk/medical-dictionary/hyperandrogenism

Only 40 percent of women who have polycystic ovaries diagnosed by an ultrasound have PCOS. The diagnosis of PCOS only says what the clinical condition is. It does not tell you about the root cause.

There have been studies looking specifically at PCOS to isolate the genetic defect. It runs in families, but so far, they have not been able to isolate a gene or a SNP (Single Nucleotide Polymorphism) that is the most common type of genetic variation among people[13]. There have been some other criteria that have a higher prevalence, but nothing that has proven causation.

There are three basic theories of the etiology of PCOS[14].

1. The abnormality starts in the pituitary gland and for some reason, there is an abnormal pulsation of LH (Luteinizing Hormone) and FSH (Follicle-Stimulating Hormone). When you have twice as much LH, your eggs get stuck in the follicular phase and never make it to ovulation.
2. It does not start in the pituitary gland; it starts with the androgens. You make high androgens and have the evidence to support it. There are two different cell lines: both the

[13] What are single nucleotide polymorphisms (SNPs)?

https://medlineplus.gov/genetics/understanding/genomicresearch/snp/

[14] Genetic Basis of Polycystic Ovary Syndrome (PCOS): Current Perspectives, https://www.ncbi.nlm.nih.gov/pmc/articles/PMC6935309/

ovary with testosterone and the adrenal gland with DHEA-S. High testosterone suppresses ovulation by making insulin an issue.

3. This theory doesn't address the starting point but refers to insulin as the root cause of PCOS. High insulin disrupts ovulation, resulting in high testosterone. The high testosterone and high insulin suppress ovulation, which is how you get anovulation (Anovulation happens when an egg (ovum) doesn't release from your ovary during your menstrual cycle) [15].

PCOS could be caused by one of the three, or all three. When we take a natural approach to PCOS, we work first on all those points, especially insulin. One of the fastest things you can do to lower your insulin is an overnight fast of 12-14 hours.

We often use supplements such as chromium, vanadium, and inositol to sensitize your body to insulin. Some patients, however, may choose to have a pharmaceutical prescription like metformin if they need a bigger push at the beginning. We give the patients the option. Option number two works on testosterone. I have some patients that have a slow Aromatase (Also called estrogen synthetase or estrogen synthase). Aromatase is

[15] Anovulation: All you need to know, https://www.medicalnewstoday.com/articles/318552

an enzyme responsible for a key step in the biosynthesis of estrogens[16].

Perhaps they do not convert testosterone to estrogen, or they have a high 5 alpha-reductase activity, which is the enzyme that converts testosterone to dihydrotestosterone[17].

You can block that enzyme either with progesterone (which is low because you are not ovulating), or with something like zinc or saw palmetto[18]. For more information, click below:

Those are natural ways you can suppress that 5-Alpha for reductase. Because of the ovulatory dysfunction, most patients with PCOS are estrogen dominant, which feeds the whole vicious cycle. Balancing their hormones with natural micronized progesterone can also jumpstart ovulation as well.

To Have Hormone Therapy or Not?

---

[16] Aromatase, https://en.wikipedia.org/wiki/Aromatase

[17] 5-alpha reductase deficiency | Genetic and Rare Diseases Information Center (GARD) – an NCATS Program (nih.gov), https://rarediseases.info.nih.gov/diseases/5680/5-alpha-reductase-deficiency

[18] Determination of the potency of a novel saw palmetto supercritical CO2 extract (SPSE) for 5α-reductase isoform II inhibition using a cell-free in vitro test system - PubMed (nih.gov), https://pubmed.ncbi.nlm.nih.gov/27186566/

I believe there are some circumstances where you need to use hormones. For example, if I had a young teenager come in who had endometriosis symptoms and estrogen dominance, my first thought wouldn't be to give her hormones. In someone that age, I prefer the use of dietary supplements, and lifestyle changes to help estrogen detoxification.

But if she was 45 years old and had her ovaries removed, she may need to take hormones. If I get a patient in 30s and she has high estrogen and low progesterone, my concern is different again. The estrogen is going to stimulate growth in the uterus and in the breasts, increasing the risk of cancer in both.

There have been times when I used micronized progesterone—a bioidentical hormone—to bring balance (because of the effect of too much estrogen). Progesterone will downregulate the estrogen receptor. Estrogen causes growth and progesterone causes apoptosis, which is cell death.

If I am genuinely concerned that they have a lot of estrogen while we are working on their estrogen detox—phase one, and phase two in the liver, also gut health in phase three (which I will explain further in estrogen detoxification)—we use hormones. However, I do not believe in using synthetic hormones, ever.

Synthetic Hormones vs Bioidentical Hormones?

Synthetic hormones and birth control pills are the commonly accepted treatment for PCOS. There are also synthetic progestins like Provera, Medroxyprogesterone Acetate (which carry different risks). Bioidentical hormones are the ones chemically and structurally the same as what our body makes.

Blocked Fallopian Tubes

That is an exceedingly troublesome issue because it is a physical impediment. Blocked fallopian tubes can be from prior ectopic pregnancy, but are mostly from infection, radiation, or an inflammatory condition. Diagnosis is usually made with a hysterosalpingogram, or during a laparoscopy.

If the fallopian tubes are blocked, we can do a Chromotubation. We shoot dye into the tubes and watch as it comes out. There isn't a supplement to fix it. If it is an autoimmune condition like CF (Cystic Fibrosis) most times, it would have come from an infection or tubal pregnancy. We could surgically repair it or bypass it with IVF.

Detoxification

Patients need detoxification after each IVF and fertility medication treatment because Gonadotropins are used for IVF. They are synthetic analogs of the FSH and LH, and by using them, you are creating super physiological levels.

More FSH means more estrogen and then there are too many eggs. The eggs are retrieved, and conception occurs outside of the uterus when the sperm and the eggs are mixed. Then the embryos are transferred back inside the uterus. The detoxification may not specifically be from the toxins, but from the effect of all those hormones in your body. Estrogen dominance causes growth in the breasts.

If you don't have much progesterone, when you have a retrieval done, they'll treat you with higher doses of progesterone to support the pregnancy until the placenta can take over. It's all bioidentical. They do not use synthetic progesterone for that, but the effects on your body can be lasting, especially if you have had all that estrogen and then don't conceive.

Having estrogen dominance over time increases your risk of diabetes, breast and uterine cancer. Studies, however, have shown that as far as ovarian cancer is concerned, there does not appear to be an increased risk from the fertility medications.

I wonder about the exposure to estrogen, though. I had six cycles of clomid, six cycles of injections, then IVF. All that estrogen definitely flared up my endometriosis.

How to Detox Estrogen

There are three phases of estrogen detoxification.

1. In the liver and is through enzymes, called cytochrome p450[19].; the ways we can support phase one are through cruciferous vegetables like broccoli, kale and cabbage. You may have to eat up to five pounds a day to make a difference, so DIM[20] or I3C[21] are supplements that could really help.

2. COMT (Catechol-*O*-methyltransferase). This form of the enzyme helps control the levels of certain hormones[22]. Supplements that support phase two are magnesium and B vitamins. Most people can tolerate them, but some people cannot. It depends on what your COMT status is. SAMe (S-adenosyl-L-methionine (SAMe) is a compound

---

[19] The Effect of Cytochrome P450 Metabolism on Drug Response, Interactions, and Adverse Effects - American Family Physician (aafp.org), https://www.aafp.org/afp/2007/0801/p391.html

[20] What Are DIM Supplements? Benefits and more, https://www.healthline.com/nutrition/dim-supplement

[21]Indole-3-Carbinol - Uses, Side Effects, and More, https://www.webmd.com/vitamins/ai/ingredientmono-1027/indole-3-carbinol

[22] COMT Gene, https://medlineplus.gov/genetics/gene/comt/

found naturally in the body. SAMe helps produce and regulate hormones and maintain cell membranes[23]have those two phases in the liver, then whatever extracted from these phases will dump into the gut.

a. Two factors can affect estrogen detoxification in the gut:
b. If you have too many bacteria which are not eliminating.
c. Your beta glucuronidase is high (your enzyme activity can go up because of bacterial overgrowth).

3. If those two happen in the liver, it puts estrogen in a package, ties the bow, and sends it into the intestine to be excreted. If you have a high bacterial count and high beta glucuronidase activity, it's like opening that box and sending all that estrone back into your circulation.

Cleaning up your diet, increasing your fibre, and calcium d-glucarate[24], are helpful (but technically is **phase three** of estrogen detoxification).

---

[23] SAMe, https://www.mayoclinic.org/drugs-supplements-same/art-20364924

[24] CALCIUM D-GLUCARATE: Overview, Uses, Side Effects, Precautions, Interactions, Dosing and Reviews (webmd.com), https://www.webmd.com/vitamins/ai/ingredientmono-136/calcium-d-glucarate

In addition, when we are talking about detoxifying, we are also talking about decreasing your exposure to estrogens in the environment. For example, plastics, chemicals in your skin care, your hair care, and in cleaning supplies, phthalates and BPA[25]. We have had some patients notice a change in their menstrual cycles simply by just eliminating Tupperware and reusable disposable water bottles.

Then there's food. Do you know how much food has extra hormones? I remember chicken breasts were far smaller than they are now. The food industry is putting hormones and toxins, or endocrine disruptors, into our environment.

So, "*The dirty dozen and the clean 15*" can be your reference list. That addresses a list of food made yearly by the Environmental Working Group to guide you on what you should avoid or eat in an organic form. https://www.ewg.org/

It's imperative for our health to eat organic and avoid foods that have a high content of endocrine disruptors and chemicals in them. So, by changing your diet and environment, and working on your estrogen load and your estrogen exposure, you're working at a cellular level.

---

[25] What is BPA? Should I be worried about it? - Mayo Clinic, https://www.mayoclinic.org/healthy-lifestyle/nutrition-and-healthy-eating/expert-answers/bpa/faq-20058331

Never Lose Hope:

I remember how desperate I was to become pregnant. I couldn't wait to do the test. But with my irregular periods, it could be 28, 35, or 40 days before I found out I wasn't. I remember waiting, feeling like I was pregnant, then finding out I wasn't. Then there was the roller coaster of the medications which made it all worse, including the birth control pills I had to take for a month because I had ovarian cysts.

If I had known what I know now, with my integrated approach to my Hashimoto's thyroiditis, gut health and estrogen detoxification, I don't think I would have a problem getting pregnant. I was even able to cure my endometriosis. So, if you're struggling, don't give up. There is hope.

I recently had a patient who was 46 years old. She and her second husband really wanted to conceive. After they had several failed cycles, we looked at her gut. She had candida, a yeast fungus. Once her gut microbiome balance was restored, and she'd completed her estrogen detoxification, she conceived. She is due to have her baby next month.

Don't give up. This multi-integrative approach works and will give you the best chance at success.

I wish you well.

Visit my Online Learning Academy for workshops, boot camps, and in-depth courses on women's hormone health at: http://hormone-guru.com

CHAPTER 5

Reversing Autoimmune Disease

By Salena Rothenberger, Functional Medicine Practitioner

My journey through life changed dramatically in 2014, when my oldest son was diagnosed with Type 1 Diabetes. This came as a huge surprise. With no family history of the illness, the diagnosis stopped me dead in my tracks. A whirlwind of thoughts and memories raced through my head of all his chronic health challenges since birth.

We'd suffered through four miscarriages. So, once we finally had a full-term, successful pregnancy and birth, we changed our diet by eating organic and homemade foods. We thought we were doing everything right.

I've always believed a momma's instinct is usually right. Mine most certainly was in the case of my son. There was a mountain of signs and symptoms. He was sick as a baby from day one, vomiting within hours of birth after eating his first meal. He had GERD

(Gastroesophageal Reflux Disease), chronic ear infections, and contracted an RSV (Respiratory Syncytial Virus). Through all of this, he failed to thrive. He developed eczema as well and battled with constipation.

"He is normal," the doctors diagnosed after countless appointments. "He will grow out of it," they said after yet another appointment.

By the time he was nine, he grew right into an autoimmune disease. It was then I realized that if we kept doing the same thing over and over, we were going to keep having the same results.

"That's it!" I said. "I'm done!" Everything we had tried right up to this point had kept me from my childhood dream of having 6 boys and 6 girls. Now, my oldest child was diagnosed with a lifelong illness. Even though we'd gone down the natural route, something was still missing. Our search to find real answers began. I wasn't allowing my mother's instinct to be dismissed any more.

Literally, we traveled from coast to coast. We saw doctors in Washington DC, San Francisco, and in between, including Texas, where we now live. Eventually, it was our family doctor who encouraged me to shift my search and dive into functional medicine. He met with me on a weekly basis to discuss my son's case. We reviewed what we were doing, what we'd learned from the other providers we'd traveled to see, and spent countless hours researching together, hoping to find the answers.

"*You're not going to find those answers in mainstream medicine,*" *he said.* "*The questions you're asking me, I wasn't taught in medical school. The answers you're searching for, you will never find them where you are looking.*" Our conversations then shifted. I would pursue functional and natural medicine.

Our doctor was the catalyst to push me past my mission to just heal my child. I went to the next level. Within a couple of weeks, I enrolled at the Functional Medicine University. In addition, I took every class I could get my hands on, such as advanced courses on immunology, autoimmunity, and genetics.

Breaking The Vicious Cycle of Miscarriage

Our fourth miscarriage was different. Something happened during that miscarriage that led me to search for doctors who performed Cervical Cerclages (Procedures like using stitches or synthetic tape to keep the cervix from opening prematurely, thus ending the pregnancy).

I narrowed it down to a few places. One was in Texas, and another was in Massachusetts. Besides the fertility struggles, my husband yearned to return closer to his home in New England. So, Massachusetts it was. We moved halfway across the country.

The approach to infertility was still mainstream medicine up to this point. We did what conventional medicine does for infertility. But on our fifth attempt as we were preparing for another IVF procedure, we found out, much to our surprise, that we'd somehow conceived.

That was interesting. We hadn't done anything different, other than **not stress** about it. We were both happy with where we were living. I contend that was the true catalyst behind us conceiving naturally.

However, there were complications. Due to the previous miscarriages, I instantly became stressed and worried that we would lose another child. Internally I was on pins and needles 24/7 and that progressed as the pregnancy went along. Towards the end of the first trimester, I received an operation for an external cerclage (despite me desperately trying to get a doctor to believe that I needed an internal one).

In the middle of the procedure, while I was lying on the operating table numb from the waist down yet fully awake, the staff started whispering in the corner. They made a lot of frantic phone calls and rushed in and out of the OR. The anesthetist was doing his very best to keep me calm, but it was the most traumatic experience of my life up to that point. My body couldn't bear the fact that something was wrong. They just wouldn't tell me what it was.

I lay there petrified, wondering if I was going to lose our fifth child. I was on the verge of hyperventilating when my doctor finally came back in.

"Your cervix has a vertical laceration from end to end," she said with a calm yet very concerning tone. It's difficult to describe the mixture of feelings I had. Instantly, I felt an overwhelming relief as *finally* my instincts were validated about the type of cerclage I needed. Then the tears flowed uncontrollably. It meant I would have another incredibly high-risk pregnancy.

Miraculously, we carried our son all the way to term. Once he was born, we decided to do everything natural. We'd do our best for our child. We made our own baby food, ate organic, and I took jobs where I could take him with me. But despite all of that, he was sick. All. The. Time. We couldn't understand why he was having so many problems.

He had reflux, ear infections, food allergies and chronic respiratory and digestive problems. At the age of nine, he was flown to Dallas Children's Hospital in a diabetic ketoacidosis (DKA) and was diagnosed with autoimmune Type 1 Diabetes. That was a defining moment for us in understanding what it really means to approach health challenges naturally.

What Would I Do Differently?

If we knew about functional medicine earlier, I would have changed the *way* we ate. Meaning, taking time to enjoy meals, eating more of a variety. We had focused on eating organic and natural food, however, we still had a very traditional standard American diet and usually ate it in a rush. Being natural and organic doesn't necessarily mean healthy. The right diet supports your body and helps heal you from the day-to-day stressors. It will produce the right hormones for your whole body, including your reproductive system.

I would also have looked at stress. I am the type of go-go personality; I do not do well with sitting and doing nothing. Instead, I excel under pressure and feel alive when I have a lot of projects on the go. Working all over the place in three different jobs didn't give me any days off. If I did have a day off at one, I worked at one of the other two.

I would have completely changed my lifestyle. I wish I had spent a lot more time doing things I enjoy. Some of my jobs were my dream jobs, so I absolutely loved those. But because I worked non-stop, I had no downtime. It was like I was a vehicle that ran a race all the time. When the race was over and it was time for it to be in the garage, I was still doing laps out on the track!

I would have looked at the different toxins in my life, especially the toxic relationships I overlooked. I've learned the importance of making sure I avoid toxins in all aspects of my life. Drugs weren't my thing, nor was smoking, and I really didn't care much for alcohol. However, there were always emotional toxins in some area of my life.

Emotional toxins are incredibly damaging and dangerous, as they tend to be silent. It took me many years, even after being in the functional medicine space, to fully understand the impact of emotional stress. Toxic relationships and childhood trauma had all been buried inside. It would have been ideal if those stressors and traumas had been addressed earlier.

Another thing I would have done differently is something that is still often overlooked in the functional medicine arena. Even though we were taking a holistic, natural, and a functional approach to our health by swapping out OTC, or prescriptions, for a herb, the reality was we were still taking the same approach! We weren't addressing the underlying reason the 'check engine lights' of our bodies were flashing!

A Shift in Lifestyle

I learned a lot about how much I neglected myself. There was no self-care. For instance, when I investigated my genetics, I discovered that I have the empathy SNP (I'm genetically more empathetic). I did a lot for others, but little for myself. Even though I was cognizant of a lot of different symptoms or distinct problems, I didn't always make myself a priority. On my journey to find answers, there was always a compromise, especially during those years, I struggled with infertility.

When my son was in the ICU at the hospital, a complete shift occurred. It changed the entire course of how I do things; how I seek answers; how I deal with situations when I don't get answers; and I process and respond (both internally and externally) when someone doesn't validate my concerns for my child. Especially if my questions are dismissed. I didn't realize I was beginning the journey down the path of self-care.

During my big shift in 2014, I thought taking this new natural approach would be simple. I thought we could get our herbs and protocols and focus on the underlying root cause. However, it was not that simple.

There were a lot of challenges in the functional and natural medicine world. I was still finding many uncertainties. I wanted a direct path that told me:

- Here's is the problem.
- Someone's going to analyze *why* it's happening now.
- Here's how you recalibrate your body to get it back on track.

Instead, what I found is:

- These are your symptoms.
- Here's your food plan.

- Here are your herbs and supplement protocol for the treatment.
- Take this three times a day and come back to me.

It was just as bad as mainstream medicine approaches. I wasn't being heard. Symptoms were dismissed, coupled with a lack of prioritizing a rebalancing of parasympathetic imbalances. There are a lot of misconceptions when it comes to natural and functional medicine. A lot of people think they can just take an herb instead of a prescription, but that is not the case.

I understand that because it's how our family practiced before my son was diagnosed. I knew there was something else out there, that something was missing. It was very frustrating because there was no individuality or customization; individuals were still being put into a box, and it just felt like I wasn't getting anywhere.

Mother's Instinct and Intuition

In the functional or natural medicine world, some key symptoms were dismissed, mainly when doctors or other health professionals couldn't understand some piece of our puzzle. There were only a few health care professionals who had a strong investigative heart and could admit when they didn't have the answers. Even fewer who were willing to help us find the solution by walking alongside us. Interestingly, they tended to be the ones who didn't shy away from probing deeper and asking questions.

"What do you think went wrong?" or "What do you think the answer might be?" There were countless times our family doctor did just that.

"Well, I am not sure what the answer is, but let's look into that together." Or "I'm not really sure. What is your heart telling you is going on under the surface?" This type of partnership helped me open my heart and follow my intuition. It was what helped make headway in changing the course of my son's health.

There's so much noise in the health space it's difficult to find the right connection with a health professional to partner with. Now, my most important mission has become validating and empowering others when their voices and instincts are not being heard. Our family doctor sat opposite me and looked me square in the eye.

"I don't think Type 1 Diabetes is curable, however, I fully believe if it can be done, you will be the one to do it." What he did for me in those few words was priceless. The only way I can repay him for that is to pay it forward.

There are countless mothers and women lying awake at night, crying. They're screaming out for help but are left feeling as though no one is out there to answer their call. Finding someone who believes in you is vital when it comes to a natural approach to healing. When you find that person, a major shift occurs.

Treating Autoimmunity Disease with Functional Medicine

When I delved into functional medicine, the first module I took had the greatest impact. It helped me realize the complexity, yet simplicity, in an approach that looks at how the body is supposed to function. The module was about GI (Gastrointestinal) health and it immediately transitioned into autoimmunity. The instructor described my child when she spoke about the mother's health pre-pregnancy, pregnancy, infancy, toddlerhood, right up to him being diagnosed with autoimmunity.

The emotions I experienced on the operating table back in 2005 resurfaced. I stopped the video while my mind raced through all the questions, I'd asked the doctors for years. I rewound the video and started it again. It was as if she had somehow known every little detail about my life; what my child experienced and then how that all led to autoimmunity.

Autoimmunity

Autoimmunity results from the body tagging self-tissue as a problem. What makes it do that? It's the million-dollar question. Every process in our body has a purpose. It doesn't just decide one day to produce antibodies to self-tissue. Rather, it is triggered by signals that alert other parts that something is where it shouldn't belong.

Much like if someone broke into your home, you'd call law enforcement. We don't just decide one day to randomly call the police department and ask them to come to our home. Nor do they just randomly imprison folks. It's the same with our body.

Asking "Why?" is at the heart of peeling back the layers of autoimmunity.

Functional and natural medicine have that same question built into their core principles. To regain balance, one must have an understanding of what is out of balance. We don't remove the check engine lights out of our vehicles and expect the underlying problem to be fixed. Instead, we see that warning light and fix the problem.

Functional and natural medicine put the symptoms into context by looking at:

- Health history
- Trauma
- Toxic exposures (including toxic relationships).
- Activity
- Sleep
- Types of foods that are fueling the body.

Taking a holistic approach like this allows us to trace the steps back to what caused the body to respond in such an aggressive manner.

Autoimmunity and Stressful Pregnancies

For most of my fifth pregnancy, I felt stressed. We'd already lived through four miscarriages, and this fifth one had an extra layer of complications. We didn't tell most of our family I was pregnant. Only those at my job and a few friends were told.

I didn't enjoy the pregnancy because I was so afraid that as soon as we told somebody, we would lose another child. That happened with all my miscarriages. I know now that all that stress transferred into my child. As I went through the functional medicine course, it was undeniably clear. My child had developed in that stressful state. It made total sense that his health would eventually lead to autoimmunity.

All the pieces completely fit because he was in this **sympathetic state** (fight-or-light mode) from the very beginning[26].

I think it was ironic that he was conceived in a **parasympathetic** state. When we weren't stressed about trying to conceive; we were completely carefree. But then, immediately upon learning of my

[26] Sympathetic vs. Parasympathetic State: How Stress Affects Your Health, https://chriskresser.com/sympathetic-vs-parasympathetic-state-how-stress-affects-your-health/

pregnancy, it shifted into an ultra-sympathetic, stressful state which played a critical role in his life, leading up to autoimmunity.

More Important than Genetics

When we looked at our family history for answers, we found zero family history of Type 1 Diabetes, and only a few that had Type 2 (because of their diet and lifestyle). I often wonder how they didn't get it much sooner. This encouraged us to keep searching for answers. For anyone diagnosed with Type 1 Diabetes, you probably know the textbook answer when you ask "Why?"

"It's due to genetics and environmental factors," the doctors will say. Yet any time one tries to probe into what those specific environmental factors are, you come up against a giant brick wall in mainstream medicine.

With my lifelong love of biochemistry, and because of my original path to veterinary medicine in college, it seemed clear there had to be something we were missing. While veterinary medicine wasn't my true calling, I believe it helped lay the groundwork for what I do now. Taking the leap into functional medicine, exploring and digging deeper into his autoimmune markers, became my top priority.

The main autoimmune markers for his Type 1 Diabetes were the zinc transporter eight (ZnT8). It is one of the least common for Type

1. The cause of his diagnosis made little sense, so we got his genetic profile and nutrigenomic testing done. Then I was able to peel back some of those layers.

I found a lot of answers to questions about why I had infertility issues, why my health was compromised, and how that led to the way his body responds (or doesn't respond) to treatment. Finding things that made him more susceptible to autoimmunity was yet another piece to our health puzzle and how our body works.

The genes we *could* do something about weren't the genes such as where my ancestors came from or how I got the color of my eyes. They were the metabolic genes, the building blocks of how our bodies process foods, and how we function. It clearly explained why I have so much empathy, and why I have problems resolving inflammation, such as my symptoms of chronic pain. It made sense of his food sensitivities and GI health challenges. Pieces of the puzzle suddenly started coming together. I realized that we actually have control over these things.

Our genes are not our destiny!

We used to believe we were born with these genes, with autoimmunity or any other chronic disease; however, this is not true. The 'environmental factors' became clearer.

Dis-ease is the effect of us being out of balance

or our organs not working in harmony.

Epigenetics vs Genomics

Epigenetics is the study of how the environment affects our body, and how, on a deeper level, our body responds to it. Epigenetics is how these building blocks are put into action and how we build our health. Do we have a tornado coming through that tears down our building? Or do we have it reinforced to withstand it?

Genomics is the study of our actual genes, the building blocks.

Nutrigenomics is looking at our genes involved in metabolic processes with a focus on nutrition. Understanding the context is the center of epigenetics and nutrigenomics. If we have genetic variants (SNPs) that make a process more difficult, we may have a lower threshold to an environmental factor much like a one-lane highway will be more susceptible to traffic getting backed up if there is an accident. It isn't always this cut and dry. Variations can have an impact on our metabolic processes as well leading to increased or decreased activity, known as gain of function and loss of function.

Where to Start Your Healing Journey?

Before going too deep, take a step back and look at the foundation of your health. If we don't have a solid foundation, everything we build upon it will fall apart. We can put the most expensive accessories in our home, but if our foundation is flawed, it's still going to fall apart. Coming back to the very core foundation is the most important thing in starting the journey to reclaiming our health.

It Starts with Laughter

This is non-negotiable. Having fun and enjoying our life activates the parasympathetic, peaceful state which is vital to our body's health and wellbeing. Make a choice to do whatever creates those deep belly-laughs until you're laughing so hard it brings tears to your eyes.

Keeping Things Simple

Another piece of the puzzle that can reduce redundancies is to declutter your mind and body from unnecessary overloads. Then you find the right answers. It is often too easy to get into the pattern of micromanaging our health until we lose sight of the simple things. This can have the greatest impact.

Connection

Connecting with somebody who can guide and mentor you is a priceless contribution to your healing. I am not talking about someone who just gives you all the answers, rather someone who is going to face the problems alongside you. Someone who will help you solve problems while guiding and teaching you how to navigate this road to health.

Transgenerational and Environmental Impact on Children

Around the time I was introduced to genetics, I noticed a pattern with my son. When I was stressed, my son's blood sugar numbers elevated. No matter how much I tried to hide it, his body could sense it. If I was having fun and enjoying my time, that also affected his blood sugar numbers. He didn't even need to be in the same room. Somehow, his body knew. It shows the impact of energy on our environment and how that can translate to other people, along with the imprinting of non-genetic stressors.

The non-genetic, transgenerational effect of the stress I experience relays to my son. His body then responds to those stresses. He is still experiencing the stress from developing inside of me for those nine months. Those stressors still play a role in how his body responds, how his genes are operating and what his body is doing now.

Solution:

I have three practical solutions that I use in my practice.

1. **Comprehensive Case Review**
    - I listen to the moms or women and their unique problems.
    - Validate those who have been trying to seek help and get answers.
    - Help them find the missing pieces not being connected.
    - Sift through the clues together and ask them what their instinct is telling them.
    - Determine if their problem is something I can help with, or do I need to point them in a different direction.

2. **Connecting Others with the right practitioners**
    - Finding practitioners who have experience dealing with the patient's specific health challenges. Ideally with practitioners have a personal experience with that dis-ease as they'll know exactly what the underlying patterns are and how they can help.
    - When it comes time for healing, I really enjoy connecting the right professionals with my clients. I've been where they are, trying to find those unique connections. It was an enormous struggle for me.

3. **Nutrigenomics.** This involves the study of how food and the environment affect a person's genes and how that person's genes affect the way their body responds to food and environmental stressors. Nutrigenomics is used to learn more about how genes and diet together affect a person's health and risk of developing dysfunction, especially in an illness like cancer and autoimmunity. It may also help find new ways to prevent and treat disease. Remember, our genes are the building blocks.

    - Look beyond genes by investigating symptoms, health history, and even the mother's history whenever she was pregnant.
    - Look at history going back as far as possible to the transgenerational component.
    - I also help others to look at their labs to discover how their body is dealing with their current challenges. What are the symptoms their body is trying to express? How is that reflected in lab results? We can put it all into context to analyze the current state of the body and where we need to go from there[27].

[27] nutrigenomics, https://www.cancer.gov/publications/dictionaries/cancer-terms/def/nutrigenomics

Free Resources

I offer several free resources on my website: https://thefunctionalperspective.com because I know many people are trying to find answers.

- **Strategy Guide** to go through the foundation of your health. This includes a free functional health score with a series of questions to give you that big, broad, 10,000-foot view of what is going on. It will also show how far they are on that continuum towards something like autoimmunity or to a lifelong disease or imbalance in our health.

- **Candida Symptom Checker**. It's online and looks at things like candida that could be an underlying cause or something fueling your health situation.

- **Quick Reference Guide** to help understand genetics. One of the 'celebrity genes' in the spotlight is MTHFR (Methylenetetrahydrofolate reductase — an enzyme that breaks down the amino acid homocysteine) which has over 4,100 studies. It's on the top ten list of most cited genes. Many supplements have changed formulas to include methylated folate (what the MTHFR gene produces in the body) to provide a form of folate that is in alignment with what the body naturally produces (instead of folic acid, which is a synthetic version). This sounds like a good thing, right? Not necessarily!

There are many more pieces and SNPs in the folate pathway and adjoining pathways, such as methionine, that must be taken into consideration. Running out and getting methylfolate because of a variant of MTHFR may not fix someone's imbalance. It can increase the dysfunction in that or other pathways. Dr. Ben Lynch has written one of my favorite books surrounding the foundations of MTHFR and exposing the problems with treating each SNP out of context[28] [29].

I've seen a lot of misconceptions and misunderstandings with our biochemical genes, like MTHFR and what we do about a SNP. I have a quick reference guide to help you understand what you

[28] MTHFR Gene - Methylenetetrahydrofolate Reductase, https://www.genecards.org/cgi-bin/carddisp.pl?gene=MTHFR&keywords=mthfr#publications

[29] Top 10 Genes in the Human Genome,

https://blog.dnagenotek.com/the-top-ten-most-studied-human-genes-of-all-time

should do, what you shouldn't do, and whether genomic testing is right for you.

Last Word

I hope anyone reading this book, especially mothers and women, will have learned to listen to your instinct. It's real and worthy to be listened to. If you haven't found the answers yet, there is hope. You still have the opportunity to find those answers through a functional, natural, or holistic approach. You can rebalance your body and seek a restoration of health and wellness.

Connect with me at:

https://thefunctionalperspective.com/schedule to share your story and start the journey of bridging the gap.

CHAPTER 6

Orthopedic Medicine

By Dr. Jordanna Quinn – Physician, Regenerative, Anti-Aging, Functional Medicine, Rehabilitation, Osteopath and Medical Aesthetics

I knew I wanted to become a physician in 7th grade. It seemed the perfect way to combine my love of science with my love of learning and being of service to others. I started with osteopathy. We went through the same rigorous medical school curriculum as the traditionally trained medical doctors, but as osteopaths also learn hands-on manipulations and adjustments. These help gain a greater understanding and respect for how human anatomy and physiology can affect many disease and pain states.

Because osteopaths go through meticulous anatomy and hands-on education, osteopathy often lends itself to taking a more holistic approach to medicine and the human body. Medical school was the typical four-year curriculum, and then a chosen residency. I chose Physical Medicine and Rehabilitation (PM&R), which added another four years of specialty training.

PM&R is the study of anything that makes you move abnormally: brain injuries, spinal cord injuries, sports medicine, pain medicine, non-operative orthopedics, cardiac rehab, cancer rehab, etc. I'd been an athlete my entire life, so understanding how the body's movement affects the whole was ingrained in my every cell. Additionally, my mother cooked every meal from scratch and preached long-term health through food and exercise. Everything I ate growing up was unprocessed and all natural. So, it made sense to me that a "natural" way of life kept a person healthy, fit, and happy.

After I completed my residency in 2010, I joined a traditional private practice performing spinal injections and sports medicine. It was during that time that I explored alternative treatments for patient care, outside of traditional steroid injections and medications.

I felt, within the depths of my being, that a more natural approach to medicine made sense for true health and healing. Through researching alternative options, I discovered regenerative medicine. I became a Regenerative Medicine specialist at an Anti-Aging Medicine practice and learned not only how to treat patients using Regenerative Medicine techniques, but I also learned the entire realm of Anti-Aging medicine.

It was in this field that I learned how to take a functional and holistic medical approach to care, and where I truly found my passion and my calling in medicine.

What Is Orthopedic Medicine?

Orthopedic medicine is the study of the musculoskeletal system and how it interacts with the rest of the body: How your muscles, nerves, and physiology interact to make your body move properly and without pain. It is called orthopedic medicine because it is an approach to orthopedics without the surgical component.

Specialists in orthopedic medicine typically use non-invasive or minimally invasive approaches to orthopedic care, helping patients improve their quality of life with less pain. Many physicians in this space use both traditional medical techniques and newer, regenerative medicine techniques. The goal of orthopedic medicine is to perform less invasive procedures than surgery. They are typically done in the office setting and do not require extended rehabilitation, lost time from work, or recovery from general anesthesia.

Athletes of all levels are great candidates for these procedures. I have treated professional football players, professional bikers, hockey players, and more. I have also treated weekend warriors, grandparents that want to keep up with their grandkids, new mothers who are breastfeeding and don't want foreign medications in their system, and even people in their 90s who are not surgical candidates due to advanced age.

How Does Regenerative Orthopedic Medicine Keep a Person Out of the Operating Room?

Regenerative medicine focuses on healing the body by using and stimulating the body's own innate healing mechanism. It establishes normal function and heals previously irreparable tissues. As people age, we accumulate micro stressors throughout our joints, ligaments and tendons, organs, and muscles. These injuries occur from just running into a wall, a small fall that we don't think twice about, or even just our daily activities as children.

Our overt injuries as a young person create tiny, long-lasting effects in the body that become noticeable as we age. While there may not be one injury that causes major dysfunction, the accumulation of these injuries can result in pain and decreased range of motion.

When we are young, we have ample healing cells in our bloodstream and tissues to help repair the damaged areas. As we age, the amount of stem cells, hormones, and other repair mechanisms we have in our tissues decreases, and our blood flow to our injured tissues declines as well. So not only do we have fewer repair cells available, those that remain don't have a great means of getting to where they need to go. Our ability to repair the injured joints, tendons, and ligaments declines, thus arthritis, pain, and chronic injury ensue.

Regenerative medicine aims to improve the body's ability to heal through a variety of mechanisms. It first causes a mechanical injury directly to the diseased tissue by introducing a needle to the area. When this happens, blood flow is stimulated to bring healing factors to the newly injured tissue. Regenerative medicine then adds a healing substance, introduced via a needle, to help decrease pain and heal the injured area. By repairing damaged tissues, we can keep patients out of the operating room and save them time and money in the long run.

My regenerative medicine patients typically walk out of the procedure room on their own, without feeling woozy from general anesthesia and without significant pain. They can go back to work the following day, and if they are professional athletes, they only take a few days off from practice. The people who have these regenerative medicine procedures typically begin noticing an improvement in their pain within a couple of weeks and are back to their regular daily activities within days of the procedure.

Types of Regenerative Medicine

There are multiple facets of regenerative medicine, but the three biggest ones for orthopedic purposes are called prolotherapy, platelet-rich plasma and mesenchymal stem cells.

PROLOTHERAPY

Prolotherapy is the original form of regenerative medicine. An administration of an irritating solution, such as sugar, is injected into a joint, tendon or ligament, to stimulate healing. The sugar solution works in combination with the injection to introduce a mechanical injury (needles) and a chemical irritant to the area. This stimulates and attracts immune cells and growth factors to the area of injury and encourages healing and tightening down of ligaments and tendons. This type of regenerative medicine is effective for lax (hypermobile) ligaments around the vertebrae, joints, or other areas. We often use this after dislocations, whiplash injury, repetitive physical traumas, and more.

PLATELET RICH PLASMA (PRP)

Platelet-rich plasma uses platelets from your bloodstream to induce a healing response within the body. Blood is drawn from the patient and processed in such a way that extracts and concentrates the platelets to a precise concentration for an injection. The platelets are then injected into the injured area under imaging guidance, either ultrasound or x-ray guidance.

This technique introduces a micro injury, as described above, and also introduces specific healing factors of the bloodstream. The physician forces a very potent and healing blood supply to an area that did not have one. Joints, ligaments, and tendons tend to have a poor blood supply on their own, and this declines even further with age.

Platelets work via a variety of mechanisms. I like to call platelets the "general contractors" of the blood. Once placed into the injured tissue, they release growth factors for improved healing. The platelets also use cell-to-cell communication to call for local stem cells in the blood and in nearby tissues to come into the injured tissue and help in the repair process.

MESENCHYMAL STEM CELLS

Stem cells exist throughout the human body and are in a constant state of evolution within their lifespans. They are circulating in your blood, and they are in your bones and your skin. They are also surrounding every tissue that is within the human body. The highest concentration of autologous mesenchymal stem cells exists in fat tissue (adipose) and in the bone marrow.

Autologous means they come from your own body, are your own stem cells. They have the ability to differentiate into multiple cell types and thus heal injured tendons, ligaments, muscles, cartilage, and more, thereby being the ideal stem cell type to use for orthopaedic[30].

As mentioned prior, tendons, joints, and ligaments have a poor blood supply, making it difficult or even impossible to heal those areas without intervention. The bloodstream is the highway to healing. Without a good blood supply, the body cannot send healing factors to an injured area. Injecting the body's own healing cells enables us to bypass the highway and directly give the injured tissues the healing factors for repair.

Mesenchymal stem cells are like the "master craftsmen" of the blood. They work together quickly to help decrease inflammation and pain. Stem cells also recruit surrounding stem cells to get in on the action of repairing the damaged tissue. They coordinate the healing process by repairing damaged tissue and cleaning up leftover inflammatory particles that were in the area.

In order to access these cells, a physician must be well trained in regenerative medicine. To extract bone marrow, the physician uses a

---

[30] Xiaorong Fu, Ge Liu, Alexander Halim, Yang Ju, Qing Luo, and Guanbin Song, Mesenchymal Stem Cell Migration and Tissue Repair. Cells. 2019 Aug; 8(8): 784, https://www.ncbi.nlm.nih.gov/pmc/articles/PMC6721499/

small trocar to get into the bone marrow along the back of the hip. She then advances it far enough into the bone to gently extract the cells. In order to extract fat cells, physicians perform a mini liposuction using a cannula technique, where they get specific fat along the flank where the highest quality adipose stem cells live.

There are other types of adult stem cells used in orthopedic medicine. These are amniotic or umbilical cord blood stem cells. These are not FDA (Food and Drug Administration) approved and have not been proven as effective as autologous use. Some labs have tested the viability of these so-called "stem cells" and have not actually found any live cells.

These types of treatments may be beneficial for a small subset of patients, but they should only be used when the patient isn't a good candidate for extraction of their own bone marrow or adipose stem cells, such as someone who has osteoporosis, so extracting bone marrow is not safe. Or someone who has a recent history of cancer.

It takes a highly trained physician to perform the bone marrow extraction, or the liposuction needed to get autologous stem cells. They alone should be trusted with deciding which type of stem cell is most appropriate for the patient's condition. If a clinic cannot offer the patient autologous stem cells as an option for treatment, that clinic and its providers are not adequately trained in regenerative medicine and should not be performing these procedures.

Each of these regenerative medicine procedures seems like they are similar and serve the same purpose. However, there are nuances as to when a physician will choose to use one type of procedure over the other. As a general rule, when a patient has extensive ligamentous laxity or mobility, I prefer to use prolotherapy.

Once a patient has significant arthritis in a joint, I think stem cells are the best treatment. PRP is great for a single meniscus tear in the knee, or a single rotator cuff tear in the shoulder. However, examining a patient in person is a very important part of the decision-making process. It ensures we know which procedure to choose. Often, the regenerative medicine procedures are done in combination with each other.

How Can Regenerative Medicine Work in Aesthetics?

The beauty of affecting change on a basic physiological and cellular level isn't just useful in a single branch of medicine. As physicians and scientists, we can understand how cellular biology works at its core and use that knowledge in other areas of medicine as well.

PRP and stem cells are used in many areas of medicine, including in aesthetic medicine (specialties that alter cosmetic appearance). PRP and/or stem cells are used intradermally and subdermally to stimulate collagen, growth factors, and healing factors in the skin. They also help decrease fine lines and wrinkles.

So, while they are not healing an injury, they are stimulating the body's natural healing response in and under the skin to help regenerate cells, have more cellular turnover, and thus look more youthful.

Regenerative Medicine uses orthopedics to focus on healing the body by using and stimulating the body's innate healing mechanisms via prolotherapy, PRP, and stem cell treatments. Another aspect of regenerative medicine exists with how patients spend their everyday lives.

What Can You Do to Improve Your Own Cellular Health?

Sleep, stress, diet, and exercise, each on their own or in combination, are extremely important for intracellular health, also, for the regeneration and optimization of existing stem cells in the bloodstream. Optimizing each of these areas of health plays a large role in daily physical and mental performance, and in how a patient responds to and recovers from the above procedures. Once you make small, daily changes in each of these areas, you will notice vast improvements in how you feel in your general health and well-being.

SLEEP

Insufficient sleep quantity or quality leads to decreases in general health, cardiovascular health, mental health, cellular health, physical performance, and more. During sleep, the body regenerates and rejuvenates. Sleep allows the body to repair damaged tissue by increasing growth hormones and stem cell production, also, by optimizing internal repair mechanisms.

Sleep helps regulate cortisol production, insulin resistance, metabolic hormone production, and more. With good quality sleep, a person actively decreases their overall mortality risk as compared to those who sleep less than 6 hours per night. Lack of sleep has been associated with poor pancreatic control of glucose regulation and with increased production of proinflammatory particles in the bloodstream.

Poor sleep leads to increased inflammation in the body, and therefore poor pain control, poor digestion, and increased risk of autoimmunity. Prolonged inflammation also increases the risk of cardiovascular disease, heart attack, high blood pressure, and more. Physical injuries do not heal as efficiently when sleep is poor. Good restorative sleep is incredibly important for stem cell production and for the overall restorative state in the body. Sleep not only affects physical health and performance, it plays a large role in mental health and cognitive function as well. As sleep time declines, mental health suffers. Lack of sleep is correlated with poor attention, decreased executive function, impaired memory, slower cognitive thought, and poor processing speed. People with chronic sleep deprivation have been shown to experience increased incidence of anxiety, depression, and other mental health[31].

Mindfulness meditation is proven to improve sleep quality and improve lifespan by decreasing ruminative thoughts and emotional reactivity. Evidence shows a decrease in stress and improvement in general health, which suggests that both sleep and stress levels play an important role in overall health, either separately or in combination with each other [32].

I found when practicing a 10–20-minute meditation each day, I could control my thoughts and my emotions, calm the stressors from the day, and relax into sleep more easily.

Improving your sleep quality and quantity will establish good sleep habits.

- ✓ Go to sleep at the same time every night.
- ✓ Avoid all caffeine after noon, as it can stay in your system for up to 12 hours.
- ✓ Exercise regularly.

---

[31] Grandner MA. Sleep, Health, and Society. Sleep Med Clin. 2017 Mar;12(1):1-22.

[32] Rusch HL, Rosario M, Levison LM, Olivera A, Livingston WS, Wu T, Gill JM.The effect of mindfulness meditation on sleep quality: a systematic review and meta-analysis of randomized controlled trials. Ann N Y Acad Sci. 2019 Jun;1445(1):5-16

- ✓ Refrain from cardiovascular exercise within 2 hours of sleep
- ✓ Don't look at screens (tablets, phone, or TV) within an hour of sleep.

If you change your habits over time and still have difficulty falling asleep or staying asleep, you may want to visit a physician to see if there are other causes, such as hormone issues or sleep apnea[33].

STRESS[34]

Stress has a major influence on mood and our general sense of wellbeing. The relationship between psychosocial stressors and physiological disease relates stress to a variety of factors, including, but not limited to, the nature of the stressor in combination with the person's ability to cope with the stressor. Prolonged stress leads to increased tissue damage, decreased cellular health, and increased disease.

---

[33]Sleep Apnea: Types, Common Causes, Risk Factors, Effects on Health, https://www.webmd.com/sleep-disorders/sleep-apnea/sleep-apnea

[34] Schneiderman N, Ironson G, Siegel SD. Stress and health: psychological, behavioral, and biological determinants., Annu Rev Clin Psychol. 2005;1:607-28.

Individuals with poor coping skills have increased and prolonged physiologic, neutral, and hormonal responses to stress. While these responses are important and protective during acute stress, individuals with prolonged and chronic stress have a higher risk of developing physical and mental health issues.

Following an acute stressor, the nervous, cardiovascular, endocrine and immune systems undergo a cascade of events. These events are important in the short term. The cardiovascular and nervous systems increase blood pressure to divert energy to the tissues that need increased distribution of energy. Stress hormones are released to increase energy stores in appropriate areas. The immune system is activated to prepare for battle. These are all important for an acute stress response but become maladaptive when activated frequently or continuously.

In chronic stress, persistently increased blood pressure may result in a stroke or a heart attack. Chronic stress causes an overactive immune system and increases the risk of acquiring an autoimmune disease. Having an overactive immune system over a prolonged period increases plaque formation in the blood vessels, inflammation in the joints (arthritis), poor response to viral/bacterial attack, and poor gut health. Prolonged inflammation also leads to feelings of fatigue, malaise, loss of appetite, and depression. Prolonged persistent and significant stressors, in combination with age, genetics, diet, exercise, consumption, and other constitutional factors, lead to an increased chance of developing physical and mental disease.

To decrease stress, I recommend taking 5-minutes out of your morning to concentrate on your breathing. Sit and focus on inhaling and exhaling. Your mind will wander, but stick to it, and over time, it will become easier. If nothing else, this is 5-minutes during the day when you are not focusing on everything in your life that is causing you stress.

I would recommend doing this once in the morning, before screens and before coffee, and once in the evening, before dinner. There is also the option of purchasing meditation apps to help you calm your mind and focus. There are meditation devices such as the Muse headband that give you immediate biofeedback to help decrease the noise in your mind, have sharper focus and a better sleep. Another excellent strategy is regular exercise. Daily, consistent exercise for just 30 minutes, helps to release endorphins and improves stress and sleep quality. Finally, a newer, and more emerging field for stress reduction, anxiety reduction, and general optimal mental capacity is the field of psychedelic medicine.

Much research is being done around the various psychedelics used to produce transformational experiences for patients with minimal numbers of treatment sessions, in order to achieve optimal mental health and decreased stress in a short amount of time. Ketamine is presently the only legal psychedelic medicine approved in the US for this purpose, but MDMA, psilocybin, and others are being researched for their powerful anti-anxiety and anti-depressive effects on patients.

DIET

Food is so important. And not just what you eat, but *when* you eat. As is your mental approach to eating. Minimizing processed foods decreases inflammation in the gut and decreases the associated risk for chronic disease and autoimmune disease.

A Mediterranean diet, specifically, has been shown to decrease cholesterol levels, protect against oxidative (inflammatory and degenerative) stress, decrease cancer risk, improve gut health, and improve insulin sensitivity. It promotes brain health, gut health, cardiovascular health, hormone health, allergy management, and more.

Eating a Mediterranean diet has been shown to increase resistance to physical and mental stress. Eating a diversity of foods from multiple different sources synergistically has been proven to help reduce inflammation and decrease risk of acquiring type 2 diabetes. "Higher quality diets", consisting of whole grains, unprocessed foods, low trans fats, and high olive oil, all have antioxidant and anti-inflammatory effects.

The Mediterranean diet increases satiety-producing hormones and, thus, secondarily, helps prevent overeating and weight gain. The Mediterranean diet helps excretion of bad estrogen in the gut, thereby decreasing risk of estrogen receptor-positive breast cancer and other estrogen-dependent cancers. It has also been shown that moderate animal protein restriction, and/or limiting animal proteins in the diet, decreases the risk of getting cancer and increases lifespan, independent of caloric intake[35].

Not only is what you eat important, but the timing of your food intake plays a significant role in health. Calorie restriction has been proven to increase longevity, promote weight loss, and decrease cancer risk. There are many types of caloric restriction diets. There are also pharmaceuticals that mimic calorie restriction, such as Feinstein and metformin[36].

Calorie restriction in the form of fasting or intermittent fasting, or even in taking medications that mimic calorie restriction, encourages cellular autophagy[37]. This is the processing and recycling of intracellular particles for degradation.

---

[35] Tosti V, Bertozzi B, Fontana L. Health Benefits of the Mediterranean Diet: Metabolic and Molecular Mechanisms., https://pubmed.ncbi.nlm.nih.gov/29244059/ , J Gerontol A Biol Sci Med Sci. 2018 Mar 2;73(3):318-326.

[36] Longo VD, Panda S. Fasting, Circadian Rhythms, and Time-Restricted Feeding in Healthy Lifespan. Cell Metab. 2016 Jun 14;23(6):1048-1059.

[37] Wong SQ, et al. Autophagy in Aging and Longevity. Hum Genet. 2020 Mar;139(3):277-290.

The better our bodies are at getting rid of dead or unwanted cells, the less potential there is for chronic and age-related diseases. People who have robust autophagic systems have been proven to have less neurodegenerative disease, cardiovascular disease, cancer, and other chronic disease. They also have improved longevity (both health span and lifespan are greater). Calorie restriction, by way of autophagy, results in better lipid levels and improved glucose control[38].

EXERCISE

Moderate running and exercise also increase autophagy and results in increased lifespan and decreased incidence of chronic disease. Exercise, specifically weight-bearing exercise and strength training, decreases incidence of osteoporosis and improves cellular production of energy. Exercise also promotes healthy expression of genes and increases the number of stem cells circulating in the bloodstream. This allows better healing and repair of damaged tissue.

Exercise improves sleep quality and sleep duration. Both cardiovascular exercise and weight-bearing exercise decrease the body's acquired stress response, mimic calorie restriction, and

---

[38] Patterson RE, Sears DD. Metabolic Effects of Intermittent Fasting. Annu Rev Nutr. 2017 Aug 21;37:371-393

improve adaptive, intracellular mechanisms for repair and recovery from stress.

Regenerative Medicine, sleep, stress control, diet and exercise, work intimately together to improve intracellular healing, overall health, and improved longevity. Think of these aspects of health like compounded interest in the financial world. The more you change your daily habits to consist of a high-quality diet, good sleep, less stress, and increased exercise, the more compounded benefit you will get from your life, your cellular health, your ability to repair and recover, and your general health. Be an active participant in each of these areas of your life while you still have your health. Then managing disease won't become a full-time job.

CHAPTER 7

Common Children's Chronic Disease

By Fiona Mao, Functional Medicine Consultant and Nurse Practitioner

My name is Fiona Mao, and I am a mother, wife, daughter, sister, functional medicine practitioner and nurse practitioner. I remember the days and nights when my daughter Fae had eczema. My husband and I would take turns caring for her. We weren't able to change her diaper without one of us holding her down. She would take any opportunity to scratch her little body. I vividly remember one particular incident when my husband and I went out for a date night and left her with my mother, only to return to find that she had scratched herself to the point of bleeding on her arms and legs.

She had quietly woken up—unbeknownst to my mom, who was in the kitchen—and started scratching, making sure to make no sound. It was as if she understood at that young age of a year old that we had a baby monitor and that is how we stopped her. Not to worry though, she has since stopped scratching and has wonderful skin, something I thought would be almost impossible, given the severity of her symptoms. This is part of the story of how I got introduced to functional medicine.

I respect the strength of both a father and mother when they work together to fight for the health of their little ones. Parenthood doesn't come in any packaged boxes with instructions. You either pull a "My parents did this", or "I read this somewhere", or "I didn't like that as a child, so I will do the opposite with my kids." Even with all these options, you still may get it wrong.

The chronic health crisis continues to grow in our society. I believe it's time to take a closer look at other ways of managing this crisis by focusing on building stronger children for tomorrow's generation. I would encourage us all to have an open mind to the simplicity of paying attention to our environment—both external and internal.

Why Do I Recommend Functional Medicine?

Functional medicine has played a huge role in my life. It not only helped me deal with my daughter's severe eczema, but it also came through for my other child who couldn't speak. We couldn't understand why this happened to us. For one, we didn't drink, never smoked, lived a very quiet life and I was in the health field! It felt like God had jokes, but I wasn't laughing.

Honestly, it is one thing to deal with a child that is struggling with chronic health issues, but it's quite another dealing with two! I remember seeing both my daughters' labs and almost everything was 'red', and their lab values were out of range. The only way I could comprehend it was through functional medicine. I have seen its powers work wonders many times over. I couldn't get my children's health to turn around and the idea of them perpetually being on medications was unacceptable to me as a mother. With integrative/functional medicine I was able to escape that reality.

Functional medicine is "root cause" medicine. It seeks to identify and address the root cause of the disease, and views the body as one integrated system, not a collection of independent organs divided up by medical specialties. —Dr. Mark Hyman

Functional medicine goes a little deeper. It investigates and treats whole systems. It is often referred to as the medicine of *why*. It looks into the *whys*. Why does my child have a high viral load?

- Why do they have a fever?
- Why do they react to certain dyes?
- Why do their symptoms recur at a certain time like every morning or every season?

While the obvious answer would be that they have seasonal allergies, it is not just about diagnosing and giving them a pill to get rid of the symptoms. It's more about *why* you have seasonal allergies and what sets off those allergens in the first place. This is what functional medicine seeks to address. It achieves this through various ways that are individualized, holistic, and scientific. It is not a one-size-fits-all plan, but a deep dive into the root cause of the disease to reverse or eliminate it.

Chronic Health and Gut health

Many of us have heard the term "leaky gut" before. It simply means increased intestinal permeability. To help you understand this, I will use an example of a balloon. Let's assume for a moment that the balloon is acting like your child's GI tract. We know balloons can inflate and deflate depending on whether the mouth of the balloon is open or shut. If a closed balloon has a hole anywhere, we know it because when we attempt to inflate it, we notice two things.

First, if there is a hole, air will keep leaking out of the balloon. Second, if the hole is large, it will not inflate at all. This is the same concept behind a leaky gut. When your child has larger than normal intestinal spaces in their gut, food leaks out through those spaces, going to unwanted territories. It is then identified as being an invasion because they don't belong there. So, the body attempts to fix the problem by sending an army of 'good guys' to deal with the invader. Then when the body is eating 'normal' food, the body rejects it because it thinks that food is going rogue (by not going through the right intestinal canal).

The opposite is true. When a balloon is filled with water, it holds all the contents because the balloon's mouth is shut and there are no holes. The same is true for our gut. When the gut is intact and the food travels its normal route, there will be no invaders and no need for alarm. So, the food is identified as a friend and no problems arise. My point is that food can either be a friend or a foe depending on the status of your child's gut.

Based on the explanation above, I believe we should pay attention to what our children eat. If your children have leaky guts, they can eat all the finest, organic, and non-toxic foods out there, but if you don't address the status of your children's gut health, this will create and add to the vicious cycle of recurring illness. Just because you are feeding them the right fruits and vegetables doesn't mean that their internal gut barrier will identify those foods as friends. The moment those healthy foods slip through and are perceived as 'rogue' for taking a gut hole detour, there will be pain that manifests itself as recurrent or chronic illness. We need to focus on ensuring that the gut is intact and maximize the benefits of feeding them with the right nutritious foods[39].

---

[39] Tracy Harris, SAFM (school of applied medicine)

Dis-ease often begins in the gut and shows up later as a dysfunction elsewhere in the body. Over ⅔ of the immune system resides in the gut, and assesses the status of our world, based on the microbes and what we swallow. The notion that "we are what we eat" is true and oversimplified. The whole picture is we are what we:

- Eat
- Digest
- Absorb
- Convert
- What does get past the cell membranes?

Let's remember, "what happens in the gut does not necessarily stay in the gut[40]".

Chronic Health and Immune Development

The immune system lives and works in every tissue and organ throughout the body. Many chronic immune-related diseases were historically blamed on bad genes[41]. Research has shown that the interaction of an individual's genes with his or her environment,

---

[40] Alessio Fasano, M.D.: The Gut is Not Like Las Vegas, https://youtu.be/wha30RSxE6w

[41] Sheila Kilbane, Healthy Kids happy moms, https://www.amazon.com/dp/B08NHX1J7V/

truly determines how the immune system matures and functions. Immune development begins before birth and a myriad of factors influence its activity, both positively and negatively, throughout the life cycle.

Preparation for the unborn child needs to begin before conception. It is not enough to start assessing one's nutritional levels when already pregnant. Just like anything in life, preparation is key. It sets the tone for the growing fetus. A pregnant woman's age, diet, lifestyle and nutrient reserves play crucial roles in fetal development. Poor quality food, toxins and stress during pregnancy can alter the development of the fetal immune system.

It is vital we pay attention to our environment. Everything we do matters and plays a role in eliminating the chronic health crisis. At birth, whether we breast feed, choose to give antibiotics for infections or live in a toxic environment, it all affects our immune function.

Contributing Factor to the Rise in Common Childhood Illnesses

We now know that there is not usually a single event that contributes to the dysfunction of the immune system, but rather a multi-layered assault on the body's main defense mechanisms that causes malfunction.

1- Poor Quality Food

Your child's body is not designed to take in 'garbage'. It is through food that they get nutrients. If all we feed our kids is carbs and food with high sugar content, how will they heal? They need to have protein for the healing, even though they can get some energy from protein. Just like if all they had was minerals, how would they have energy to play without carbs? What about vitamins and minerals?

Not having a balanced diet matters. Feeding our bodies with junk food like cookies and ice cream leaves our children overfed but under-nourished. That makes it hard for our children to be healthy.

As Tracy Harris always says, "None of us have a back-up nutrient pantry in our left butt cheek." Our food choices matter. We need essential nutrients from our food, brought in through the GI tract, to run every cell in the body.

2- Toxins

Toxins can be both natural substances and man-made substances[42]. Man-made toxins like synthetic commercial chemicals and cigarette smoke are unwanted. They are able to mimic hormones, cause inflammatory reactions, and have direct suppressant effects on the

---

[42] Immune Foundations Patient Handbook, https://www.lifestylematrix.com/immune-foundations-patient-handbook-pack-of-10-/

immune function. With toxins present in food, water and air, our exposure to toxins is inevitable.

Examples of toxins:

- Heavy metals - Found in tobacco products, household detergents, fertilizers.
- Volatile compounds and solvents - in paint, gasoline, harsh cleaners, cigarette smoke.
- Dioxins - in petroleum derived chemicals, pesticides, and herbicides.
- Phthalates and Parabens - in lotions, soaps, toothpastes, and fragrances.

3- Stress

I'm pretty sure many mothers will relate to the stress the birthing process brings. It's been over 6 years now and I still remember being in labor at the hospital and what the labor and delivery nurse casually mentioned.

"Your baby has no hair." I was on the monitors, so I never thought anything of it. My OB-GYN doctor came in and assessed me and said the same thing.
"Wow, Fiona, your baby girl has no hair." I thought that was odd.

I was a nurse at the time, yet I forgot to ask them to assess for fetal positioning, I'm pretty sure it's because I was stressed from the labor. Unfortunately, the nurse and the doctor both failed to assess her positioning.

So, there I was, pushing and then my daughter defecated and, before I knew it, I had over 20 people in the room, mostly doctors and interns. The doctors started arguing about whether I should go for a C-Section and how that would be risky because the child's buttocks had already engaged, and the child was now at risk.

Both my mother and mother-in-law went into crying and praying mode, with my mother kneeling as she prayed while my mother-in-law stood and prayed. This was all happening as the doctors deliberated over what to do.

I was so stressed; it took me more than a month to stop crying from that traumatic experience. My daughter came into this world in such a stressful manner, and it wasn't long before my husband and I learned the consequences from the severity of her birth trauma.

For a while, I was angry and wanted to sue them. If they had checked for her fetal position, they would have known she was breech, and that they were feeling her buttocks and not her head. So, I had a breech vaginal delivery in a hospital that had a NO-breech-vaginal-delivery policy. Everything went wrong that day except for the fact that she made it. I remember how my husband tried to comfort me as best he could, but I was inconsolable.

I share this story because for so long, I thought I was the one stressed out that day, not paying attention to the stress that my daughter experienced. How many mothers take into consideration how much stress their fetus experiences during labor? How many parents remember that the fetus can experience stress while in the womb? On our healing journey, my daughter and I actually took remedies together to help us heal from that experience.

Parents should take into account that children also get stressed. I think as adults, this may not even cross our minds [43]. At its core, stress is really a force, a pressure and we can all deal with it relatively well. The problem comes when it is prolonged. We tend to stay in a sympathetic (fight or flight) mode, rather than parasympathetic (relaxation) mode.

Whenever a child has a traumatic experience, gets recurring infections, or slow wound healing, all of these can be exacerbated by stress. Chronic stress, if not managed early, taxes the body and interferes with our health. This makes it hard for the child to tackle healing.

We all struggle with stressors every day. As parents, we need to focus on giving our children more calming experiences and this is, so they don't dwell in a stressful environment for a long duration of time and end up with chronic stress that decreases their rate of healing.

---

[43] Sheila Kilbane, Healthy Kids happy moms, https://www.amazon.com/dp/B08NHX1J7V/

Terminology to Note

- A true food allergy is mediated by the immune system like eggs or nuts.
- Food sensitivity is an inflammation created by food, but not a true allergy.
- Food intolerance is inflammation along the GI tract, which is mediated by food, but not a true allergy.
- Histamine intolerance is a reaction to foods that increase histamine levels, where the body is not efficiently able to break down and clear the histamine.

Things to Ponder When Dealing with Chronic Kid's Health

Diet: There are several diets out there. So how do you pick the one that will work for your child? How do you know you are not limiting important nutrients that they may need?

There are really 2 types of diets and 2 methods that can help.

1-Test out the Gluten Free/Casein Free (GF/CF) Diet

I would encourage any parent who has a child with recurring common illnesses like asthma, eczema, or ADHD, to attempt elimination of gluten and dairy (casein) from the child's diet for a while. I would encourage you to do this methodically and to eliminate one at a time. Pay close attention to the changes that occur when you have dropped the offending food. If you attempt both at the same time, it will make it hard to know which one worked and which one failed. If there is no change in symptoms - like no improvement in their skin, improved focus, fewer episodes of wheezing, then this was not effective, and those foods can be reintroduced back into their diet.

2-Elimination or Testing Method.

When I talk of an elimination diet, this is not a permanent situation, but a temporary one. The elimination is necessary to reduce the inflammation in the gut. If you notice unwanted reactions to healthy food, for example, a banana, you need to eliminate it. For this to work, you will need to be studious in observing what foods trigger reactions in your child.

There are tests that can be done when you work with a functional medicine practitioner. These tests focus on a wide range of things, from food sensitivities to heavy metals, to assessments of parasites, and the list goes on. Remember, food sensitivity tests are different from food allergy tests. Food allergies means it could turn into a deadly situation if not handled immediately. This is where epi-pens come in handy.

A food sensitivity is a delayed reaction that may show up within minutes or even days later. Because the response does take time to appear—be it brain fog, itchy skin, bloating, mood swings—it may not be easy to identify the offending foods. You can easily test to identify what may be contributing to the unwanted reactions or behaviors exhibited by the child.

As a functional medicine practitioner, I can work with you in my group program and get the labs sent to you or you can purchase some labs from my store. For further information and assistance, go to my store at https://fionamao.mindsharecommerce.com

Remember, you only want to eliminate the offending foods to enhance the rate of healing. It is only of benefit if we are able to reduce the overall inflammation that comes from eliminating the offending food.

What also poses a challenge is that it could be anything from dust mites to pollen, to fruits, or dyes in a juice box. Therefore, I would encourage testing to narrow down the culprits. I want to point out that there isn't a test that is 100% accurate. There may be some things that are not captured. The benefit of testing is to quickly identify a whole list of foods, as opposed to manually figuring it all out with every meal.

Using both testing and elimination of known food offenders is most likely going to yield better results. We focus on elimination to bring down the inflammation load so the body can start to relax and heal. As opposed to being on alert due to inflammation. This is something many parents find daunting and why I often recommend working with a functional medicine practitioner.

Supplements

Parents often ask me if children need supplements. To those parents, my response is that it begins with the soil. Normally, you can't guarantee the soil where the food was grown was mineral and nutrient rich. If it was, you wouldn't need supplements or nutraceuticals. However, soil erosion has transpired over the years, and chemicals and fertilizers have been sprayed on the soil and plants. It's, therefore, very hard to guarantee the food you eat has all the nutrients needed.

Besides, you would have to drastically change your lifestyle to accommodate the cooking and farming needs required to pull this off. For working parents like myself, supplements are a lifesaver as they step in the gap and deliver what is lacking.

I encourage everyone to be very vigilant when it comes to taking supplements. You want to treat supplements just like you would medications. You need to have guidance on how to take them. I break this down for you in my store at https://fionamao.mindsharecommerce.com

Please also remember that the quality of what you take matters. A supplement that is loaded with sugar may be causing more harm than good. Some supplements, just like food, have gluten. You want to ensure that the supplements you are using are aligned with what you are trying to achieve. If you want to stay off gluten, ensure you aren't supplementing with gluten-rich supplements.

Some Key Supplements[44]

Zinc is an important micronutrient used by the body to enhance antioxidant defenses. It is in high demand for infections yet may become deficient during conditions that stress the immune system like a chronic infection.

Selenium is a powerful antioxidant used to protect the body from oxidative stress. Inflammatory conditions and chronic stress may deplete selenium levels.

Glutathione is the body's most powerful antioxidant. Studies have shown intracellular glutathione levels can rapidly decrease during infections, leading to a reduced ability of immune cells to fight infection.

Vitamin D is a hormone-like nutrient that plays a critical role in immune health. Vitamin D is produced in humans when the skin is exposed to direct sunlight. It can also be found in oily fish such as sardines, mackerel, and salmon. Seasonal climates and working indoors can limit exposure to sunlight, therefore supplementing with vitamin D is often essential to maintain adequate levels.

Probiotics enhance the immune system. They support the gut wall barriers, thereby decreasing gut permeability. They support the

---

[44] Immune Foundations Patient Handbook, https://www.lifestylematrix.com/immune-foundations-patient-handbook-pack-of-10-/

immune system by increasing immune cell activity and antibody response, which may be especially helpful for those with allergies.

The list is long, and I have not covered all the supplements that one may need. Remember, the supplement you need will depend on what you want to achieve for your child. A good quality multivitamin with minerals is always a good place to start. The supplements I carry at my store are vetted supplements. Also, if your child is struggling with chronic health issues, you are welcome to send an email to support@fionamao.com.

For more health tips visit my Facebook and Instagram channels @fionamaonp.

Conclusion

We are living in one of the best times ever because knowledge is readily available, and if we apply it, we will have better outcomes. Please remember that you don't have to do this alone. Know that your child's health can be both optimal and robust. Seek guidance and support from those who have gone before you.

Functional medicine has blessed the world with the knowledge that no part of the body stands alone. Our body is inter-connected and hence we need to pay attention to all systems rather than just the one that is currently affected.

To neutralize the problems, let's remember to eliminate low-quality food, toxins, and stress from our little or big babies. Let's take the time to assess what we put in their bodies and not shy away from supplements. Because life happens, we may not be able to do it all. But there is a system, with steps on how to get this done. I wish you the very best as you take charge of your child's health.

CHAPTER 8

How Energy Affects Health

By Christi Clemons Hoffman, MA, CHt

Lifelong intuitive, Channel, Teacher, Consultant, and Host of the *Radiate Wellness Podcast* and *Real-Life Angel Encounters Podcast*

My journey with infertility and digestive issues began between 2000 and 2005. It led me to numerous discoveries about my health and body: irritable bowel syndrome, food sensitivities, early menopause, Epstein-Barr, and autoimmune thyroid disease.

However, the end of my marriage in 2009 was the catalyst for my true journey. I embarked on a course of discovery into the emotional and energetic causes behind these issues. I learned how to channel my higher self and my guides. This led me to learn more about our physical bodies and the life-force energy that runs them, called *chi*, or *ki*, through the use of Reiki, a form of energy healing originating in Japan, and Quantum Healing Hypnosis Technique (QHHT) developed by Dolores Cannon. Through my years of study and practice, I have repeatedly seen how thoughts, emotions, beliefs, and trauma are at the heart of all physical dis-ease.

We speak about the circulatory system, the respiratory system, the musculoskeletal system, and all the other physical systems of the body. But we ignore what runs these systems: the energy system, composed of the seven principal chakras, the network of minor chakras, and the aura.

How Energy Affects the Body

To understand how the energy system works, imagine the body as a garden hose. When the hose is straight and un-kinked, the flow of water is unimpeded and strong. When the hose becomes kinked, springs a leak, or goes uphill, however, we can have a disruption. Similarly, when our energy system becomes kinked (blocked), leaks (overactive), or is off balance, the body, mind, and spirit do not receive the flow of wellbeing that keeps us in wellness.

The energy system becomes blocked or out of balance by what we feed it. Our thoughts and beliefs—even those learned or passed down from parents or the community—create energy. Positive thoughts and beliefs create positive energy, negative thoughts and beliefs create negative energy. We can clearly feel the difference! When our thoughts and beliefs are out of alignment with our highest and best good, they create disharmony within us. When this happens, the higher self, the larger part of ourselves, also called the soul or spirit, wants to get our attention.

Negative emotions—anger, fear, sadness, resentment—are the first indication that something is off. We need to adjust how we think or what we believe about a situation. Then, if we act accordingly and take positive steps to heal our thinking or negative beliefs, we grow and release the negative energy.

If not, the knock gets louder. The energy system experiences blockages and imbalances or becomes overactive. We feel out of sorts, fatigued perhaps, or even over-active or achy. We can stay at this stage indefinitely. But if we continue the stream of negative thoughts and beliefs, we may experience dis-ease. To understand how this works, let's look at the energy system.

The Energy System

Quantum physics tells us that at an atomic level, everything is energy. Physical matter and energetic matter are just energy that vibrate at different frequencies. Thoughts, emotions, and beliefs also convey energetic frequencies.

The energetic field around the body is called the *aura*, also known as the *auric field*, or the *energy body*. The aura surrounds the physical body 360°, approximately three to nine feet, depending on whether we're feeling open and expansive or introverted and withdrawn.

Meridians carry energy throughout the body, and the *chakras* are energetic centers within the body. Each chakra corresponds with a color, an area of core thoughts and beliefs, and a location within the body. As energetic centers, the chakras are not physical, and they are not something that can be seen in an MRI or X-ray. We can imagine them as spinning wheels of energy that extend out both the front and the back of the body. Trained energy healers and medical intuitives can feel and see them.

Below is a brief overview of each chakra. This information come in part from *Chakras Activity Book & Journal* by Knock Knock Publishing and chakras.info[45].

Root Chakra

Location: Tailbone and sitting area

Color: Red

The Root chakra is concerned with trust, security, grounding, and having physical and material needs met. Root chakra problems can stem from disruption in the family, a distant parent, poverty, trauma,

---

[45] Chakras Activity Book & Journal: Get Grounded, Feel Good, Free Your Chi & Lots of Other Cool Magical Stuff
https://www.amazon.com/dp/1683492366

job loss, etc. Physically, the Root chakra governs the feet, knees, hips, spine, intestines, legs, rectum, genitals, and tailbone.

When the Root chakra is blocked or imbalanced, we can experience obesity, hemorrhoids, constipation, sciatica, bladder issues, trust issues, security issues, “spaciness,” or food issues.

You can bring balance by:

- Wearing or eating the color red
- Eating root vegetables
- Using obsidian or garnet stones.

Also using essential oils:

- Cedarwood
- Frankincense
- Patchouli
- Vetiver.

Also, by writing or speaking affirmations, such as:

- *I am safe.*
- *I love being in my body.*
- *I can release fear and trust.*

Sacral Chakra

Location: Between the navel and the pubic bone

Color: Orange

The Sacral Chakra is concerned with creativity, passion, relationships, sexuality, and feelings of gender identity. Sacral chakra issues can arise from sexual trauma, internalized messages about gender and sexuality, and suppressed creativity. The organs and areas associated with the Sacral chakra are the bladder, lower back, testes (testicles), uterus, ovaries, fluid functions, kidneys, and the urinary tract.

Sacral chakra dysfunction is linked to creative blocks, low back pain, infertility, sexual dysfunction, emotional stability, depression, or allergies.

You can bring balance by:

- Wearing or eating the color orange
- Carnelian or citrine stones.

Also with essential oils:

- Bergamot
- Jasmine
- Sweet Orange
- Ylang Ylang.

You can also write or speak out affirmations, such as:

- *I am comfortable expressing sexuality.*
- *I embrace the pleasure of life.*

<u>Solar Plexus Chakra</u>

Location: Below the ribcage

Color: Yellow

The Solar Plexus chakra governs personal power, balance, and will. Solar Plexus imbalance and blocks arise from not standing in your power, giving power away, and being generally out of balance. We also hold fear in this chakra. Physically, the Solar Plexus chakra is connected to the stomach, digestion, gallbladder, pancreas, liver, diaphragm, metabolism, and small intestine.

When the Solar Plexus chakra is out of balance, we can experience control issues, stomach ulcers, upper GI problems, fatigue, anxiety, inaction, hypersensitivity, diabetes, blood sugar disorders, and nervousness.

You can bring balance by:

- Wearing or eating the color yellow.
- Amber or topaz stones.

With essential oils:

- Basil Cedar.

- Lemongrass.
- Vetiver.

Also, you can write or speak out affirmations, such as:

- *I have all that I need within me.*
- *I unconditionally accept myself.*

Heart Chakra:

Location: Heart, lungs, and breasts

Color: Green or sometimes pink

It should be no surprise that the Heart chakra is where we hold love, compassion, concern for loved ones, and grief. The function and organs of the body governed by the Heart chakra are breathing, lungs, circulation, heart, arms, hands, fingers, ribs, immune system, and the thymus gland.

Dysfunction in the heart chakra is linked to lack of self-love, lack of compassion, cardiac/lung problems, trust issues, depression, high blood pressure, lethargy, and the immune system.

You can bring balance by:

- Wearing or eating the color green.
- Rose quartz and peridot stones.

With essential oils:

- Geranium
- Neroli
- Rose
- Sandalwood.

Also, you can write or speak affirmations, such as:

- *I love and accept myself just the way I am.*
- *I choose compassion over judgement.*

Throat Chakra

Location: Sinuses to shoulders

Color: Turquoise

The throat chakra's primary function is communication and self-expression—in any form. This chakra is connected to integrity, speaking one's truth, holding our words back, and the feeling of having a "voice". The organs and structures the Throat chakra affects are varied: throat, jaw, lower neck, vocal cords, thyroid, mouth, parathyroid, shoulders, and lymph glands.

Blocks and imbalances in the Throat chakra can result in creative blocks, sore throats, colds, thyroid issues, infections, speech disorders, mood swings, and hormonal problems.

You can bring balance by:

- Wearing the color turquoise or light blue
- Turquoise or Larimar stones.

With essential oils:

- Bergamot
- Clary Sage
- Peppermint
- Rosemary
- Sandalwood.

Also, you can write or speak affirmations, such as:

- *I embrace integrity.*
- *I speak up for myself.*

Brow (Third Eye) Chakra:

Location: Middle of the forehead

Color: Indigo

The Brow chakra is the seat of intuition and is responsible for inspiration, memory, and mental functioning. It governs the eyes, ears, nose, brain, pituitary, cerebellum, and autonomic nervous system. Brow chakra issues can arise from ignoring intuition and holding rigid spiritual beliefs.

Dysfunction in the Brow chakra can cause headaches, insomnia, nightmares, vision problems, dizziness, nervous breakdown, headaches, and earaches.

You can bring balance by:

- Wearing the color dark blue or indigo
- Lapis, lazuli or labradorite stones.

Or with essential oils:

- Frankincense
- Juniper
- Lavender
- Patchouli.

Also, you can write or speak affirmations, such as:

- *I am open to inspiration.*
- *I listen to my inner guidance.*

Crown Chakra:

Location: Crown of the head.

Color: Violet

The crown chakra is the seat of our understanding and our spiritual center. It is where we carry our connection to the higher self. Physically, the crown chakra rules the skull, skin, upper brain, pineal gland, cerebral cortex, central nervous system, and the top of head.

Blocks in the crown chakra can result in isolation and loneliness, closed-mindedness, and indecision.

You can bring balance by:

- Wearing or eating the color purple
- Amethyst or selenite stones.

With essential oils:

- Cedarwood
- Clary Sage
- Frankincense
- Lavender.

Also, with affirmations such as:

- *I am connected to all that is.*
- *I am inspired each and every day.*

Chronic Negativity and Negative Beliefs

It's important to note that one bad day or one negative thought does not result in pain or dis-ease. The chronic *patterns* of thought—or negative emotions—are what can cause physical symptoms. It can even be the messages we received in youth that we internalized.

This is also evident in "inherited" illness. What's passed down from grandparents and parent to child are patterns of thought, emotion, and belief. Over generations, these thoughts, emotions, and beliefs become solidified in the family's energetic system and even into the DNA.

This is how adopted children can take on the "inherited" illnesses and dis-ease of their adoptive family and how, though biological siblings have the same genes, genetic issues are not present equally in all children. Just because there is a genetic predisposition does not mean that it must be expressed. And sometimes we can present with an illness that no one in the family shares.

When I'm working with a client, I will usually "see" the origin of dis-ease and injury. We then discuss how a move or the loss of a grandparent at an early age, women not being allowed to speak up in the family, or love not being openly given, shows up in the body. This does not heal the body immediately, but awareness of the energetic origins of issues in the body will allow us to begin the emotional healing necessary to clear it.

Two Sides of Healing

For this reason, I like to think of healing a physical issue, like digging a tunnel through a mountain. Having spent some time in Switzerland, I traveled through many mountain tunnels by car and rail. The following diagram illustrates. On one side of the mountain, we "tunnel through" with all the appropriate medical treatments: scans and x-rays, medications, diet, therapy, etc. But on the other side, we must "tunnel through" by addressing the emotional and energetic causes contributing to the issue. Working simultaneously, we meet in the middle to achieve healing.

If we only address the medical side of healing, we will get there eventually. But we are constantly creating more issues as we go if we haven't dealt with the negative thoughts and beliefs. I might add, we have physical bodies and physical issues; it makes sense to use physical means for healing. There is a place for medical treatments and pharmaceuticals! Antibiotics, other medications, and surgery are all life-saving interventions.

By the same token, if we only address the emotional and energetic side of healing, we will also get there eventually—but if the issue took X years or generations to develop, it may take at least that long to resolve energetically alone.

It's necessary to use energy, emotional, metaphysical healing, and awareness alongside traditional medical help, meeting in the middle of the proverbial mountain.

One client I worked with had kidney stones. She was in tremendous amounts of pain. I was able to pinpoint the energetic cause as the anger she was holding in the solar plexus chakra. This is the seat of personal power and where we commonly store anger; in the client's case, it was toward her father. The client was surprised but confirmed the long-standing anger she held.

She acknowledged the emotion and replaced her negative thoughts toward her father with affirmations such as, "My father did the best he could because of how he was raised. He did not know the pain he was passing along to me."

I then flowed Reiki energy through her body, and she reached out to me the next day to tell me she'd passed the stones that night, 100% painlessly.

Another client came in for a Quantum Healing Hypnosis Technique session. She had been suffering with allergies, a throat chakra issue, for most of her life. The youngest child, and the only girl in a family of five brothers, her higher self (called the Subconscious, or SC in QHHT) told her the allergies came from feeling lost in the shuffle, unheard/unappreciated by her family, also a throat chakra issue.

Her SC further showed her many instances in her life that proved her brothers and parents adored her and appreciated what she had to say. This awareness allowed her to release a great deal of her allergies naturally.

The Role of Trauma in Illness and Dis-Ease

When working with a client, I also ask what was happening in their life when the issue arose. This helps pinpoint the mind-body connection associated with life events. Trauma within the body, whether it's physical trauma from an accident or injury, verbal trauma from a family member or friend, sexual trauma, or other form of abuse, even ancestral trauma, leaves an energetic imprint that we hold within the body.

One such example is a woman I met at a holistic wellness expo in the Kansas City area a few years ago. I had a table with Radiate Wellness, the group practice I began in 2016. After I explained the mind-body connection and my work as a medical intuitive, she asked if I could help her with something. She told me she had an eye condition and would eventually lose her sight. When I asked what was going on in her life when this condition first presented, she said that her then-teenage son was starting to get into trouble: hanging out with the wrong crowd, joy riding, petty theft, etc.

"I am a therapist for adolescents," she said. "So, I know the problems that type of behavior can lead to, and *that was not the vision* I had for my son." Sadly, this woman did not follow up with me, but I hope the realization that her vision troubles began with what she did not want to see, helped her heal the issue.

Past-life trauma can also play a big part in the mind-body connection in the present life. We hold on to fear, injustice, and trauma until we release it. This is especially true when we meet a violent or otherwise untimely death and therefore do not have the time to work through or release the heavy emotion associated with it.

The most vivid case study I have for this is a QHHT client who came in for healing from debilitating migraines. She could not work or take care of her home or family because of them. In her session, she went back to a past lifetime as a paperboy, aged eight to eleven, in a big city during the Depression. This boy lived in a walk-up apartment and was the only one in a family of four bringing in any income. That life was tragically cut short when the boy was hit by a car. After his tragic death, he continued to hang around the family for a time, fearful about what would become of his parents and baby sister.

When I brought the client out of hypnosis, she said she'd seen the entire accident. She experienced the impact, seeing a flash in her head. She pointed to the spot where the car had hit her. I asked where her migraines started; she looked shaken and pointed to the same spot on her head. She did not have another migraine for years.

Each time she felt one coming on, she talked with the paperboy and assured him that his family was ok, that he was ok, and that she would take care of him. The migraine would then stop.

Conclusion and Resources

As stated previously, understanding the energy system, the nature of trauma, and the mind-body connection will not always heal physical issues immediately. QHHT can often result in instantaneous healing, and I have seen evidence of this in my sessions, but healing can also begin in a session and continue over time. When we understand the nature of our pain and illness, we begin the process of letting it go.

I want to close this chapter with some resources I use in my practice. The body is an effective message system, and it is helpful to know where different energies and emotions are stored within it.

Soul Speak: *The Language of Your Bo*dy - by Julia Cannon, daughter of the famous Dolores Cannon, who developed QHHT. I use this frequently.

You Can Heal Your Life - by Louise Hay.

Messages from the Body: *Their Psychological Meaning* - by Dr. Michael A. Lincoln.

Each book sheds light on what we hold and where and is invaluable in deciphering physical illness and dis-ease. Above all, know that once you know where illness originates, you can begin the work of releasing it.

Epilogue
Pantea Kalhor

Thank you so much for reading our book and allowing us to share our insights into integrative medicine and mind-body connection healing with you. I invited the specialists to help write this book so we can share our real case studies and give you true and practical information about how to recover from chronic pain. You cannot find this information through Google or in any other books.

The world suffers from so many chronic diseases these days, that may lead to repetitive consumption of some medications for a long period and create a temporary relief from pain without searching for the actual root cause. This book is the professional evidence of how we can fill the gap between conventional and holistic medicine and how lifestyle can reverse most chronic diseases.

Some deaths can be easily avoided if we know how to find healing opportunities in our body and don't try to only remove our symptoms by taking pills. We can go deeper and look at the body as a whole. We also need to learn that our body, our mind, and spirit are connected to each other and so treating the physical body demands an understanding of this binding.

I hope this book has helped you create a vision and plan for your future, a way out of the anxiety, suffering pain and torture that can come as a consequence of chronic pain. May you be armed with enough knowledge to continue with your healing journey.

If you have a story that can inspire others to rebuild their life again, please connect with me at http://acechoiceidea.com.

Pantea Kalhor

About the Authors

This book is collated and published by Pantea Kalhor and AceChoice Publishing and Branding.

Other authors are Reed Davis, Dr. Defne Nayman, Fiona Mao NP-C, Dr. Jordanna Quinn, Salena Rothenberger, Dr. Tara Scott and Christi Clemons Hoffman

Pantea Kalhor,

Publisher, 4 x Best-Selling Author, Certified Fertility and PTSD Coach, Show host and Podcaster

Pantea Kalhor is the author of PTSD *Compass*, *Naturally Conceived, Rules of Change for the Better* and co-author of *Empowering Women to Succeed: Leap*. Her mission is to create a bridge between western and eastern medicine to show how holistic medicine and mind-body connection can help conventional medicine to find the underlying health issues which are usually ignored or left undiscovered.

Pantea Kalhor

She was suffering from PTSD after her car was hijacked and she was threatened by knifepoint, she started her journey of transformation. Years later, she wrote her first book Rules of

Change for The Better, describing her own personal stories of transition. Then she created Transition by Pantea Kalhor, a podcast with interviews with health care and holistic medicine practitioners, medical doctors, functional medicine practitioners, and PTSD coaches. They share the message of hope and introduce different modalities in Post Trauma recovery and healing from chronic disease.

If you wish to share your message, you can contact Pantea through her website:

https://acechoiceidea.com

If you need to consult about your fertility issues, please visit my website here:

https://panteakalhor.com

If you suffer from chronic disease or PTSD and in need of some empowerment, follow me on social media.

Facebook: https://www.facebook.com/panteakalhorcoach

Instagram: https://www.instagram.com/panteakalhorcoach

YouTube:
https://www.youtube.com/c/PanteaKalhorTransitionChannel

Podcast: https://panteakalhor.libsyn.com/

Reed Davis

Founder of FDN (Functional Diagnostic Nutrition) Certification Course, Board-certified Holistic Health Practitioner (HHP) and Expert in Functional Lab Testing and Natural Protocols

Reed Davis, Founder of FDN Reed is a board-certified Holistic Health Practitioner (HHP) and expert in functional lab testing and natural protocols. He founded Functional Diagnostic Nutrition® (FDN) and the FDN Certification Course after serving as the Case Manager at a Wellness Center in Southern California for over ten years.

Reed Davis

Having helped over 10,000 clients, Reed is known as one of the most experienced clinicians anywhere. He now serves on the American Natural Wellness Coaches Advisory Board and the

American Association of Natural Wellness Coaches. Reed lives in the U.S. teaching his course and helping graduates build their businesses or may be found gardening or riding his motorcycle.

http://www.FDNthrive.com

Dr. Defne Nayman

MD, Anti-Aging, Functional, & Metabolic Medicine, Esthetics, Mind-Body Healing, Breathwork

Dr. Defne Nayman is the Anti-Aging doctor for high-achieving women who would like to get their energy back, roll back some years, or lose weight without having to stress about it. Dr Defne has been an emergency medicine physician for over 25 years and have seen the deficiencies in the conventional medicine.

Dr. Defne Nayman

Her clinical and personal experiences prompted her to look for holistic avenues so she could help people live their lives to their fullest potential. She is currently board certified in Antiaging Medicine, Esthetics, and Emergency Medicine. DrDefne is very passionate about utilizing the tools she studied to make a difference in the lives of others. As a mind-body healer, she uses breathwork with her clients.

https://drdefne.com

Dr. Tara Scott

MD, Gynecologist, Functional Medicine Practitioner

Dr. Scott has been in front of an audience since she was the president of speech team in high school. This evolved into educating the community on hormone therapy, having taught doctors in five continents about an integrative approach. With over 20 years' experience practicing OB/GYN, and additional training in Integrative and Functional medicine.

Dr. Tara Scott

Dr. Scott shares a wealth of information by lecturing around the community to raise awareness about wellness and preventative health for patients. Having watched people suffer for years with little to no relief after countless visits to multiple healthcare providers, Dr. Scott knows how exhausting this can be.

She has lived it as a patient and seen the benefit of finding answers to the core issues. Speaking helps her reach more people in less time, helping them conquer chronic health issues. Dr. Scott's humor and analogies make complex health concepts easy for the audience to understand and put into action in order to enjoy optimal health. In addition to being the Medical Director of Integrative Medicine at Summa Health in Akron, OH, she is also the Chief Medical Officer and founder of Revitalize Medical Group, a wellness practice. She is triple board certified in OB/GYN, Functional Medicine and Integrative Medicine. She is a mother of 3 college-age children, enjoys running a half marathon in every state, traveling and being active outside.

https://drtarascott.com

Academy: http://hormone-guru.com

FaceBook: https://www.facebook.com/drtarascott/

Instagram: https://www.instagram.com/drtarascott/

TikTok: https://www.tiktok.com/@hormoneguru

YouTube: https://www.youtube.com/c/TaraScottMD

Salena Rothenberger

Functional Medicine Practitioner

Known for her intuitive investigative skills, Salena Rothenberger, D.PSc, CHC, CFMP, and her team at The Functional Perspective, combine functional health and wellness with natural methods to obtain optimal health. Dedicated to an approach of discovering imbalances and investigating health recognizes that a life full of vitality depends on resolving the root causes of dis-ease.

Salena Rothenberger

Salena Rothenberger helps moms and women find the pieces of the puzzle their instincts are searching for regarding their chronic health challenges. She works with them to explore functional, natural, holistic health approaches intertwined with nutrigenomics.

https://thefunctionalperspective.com

Fiona Mao

Functional Medicine Consultant and Nurse Practitioner

Fiona helps parents overcome the lack of knowledge and dependence on medication for their children while guiding them and their children to their desired health outcomes. Mao is the creator of Elevate Health Now, a black female-owned virtual health consulting business that focuses on functional medicine modalities and helps parents know how to manage their children's chronic health challenges.

Fiona Mao, NP-C

After assisting two of her children to recover–one who had speech challenges and another with severe allergies and eczema–Mao uses her experience to help other mothers recover their loved ones and themselves from personal chronic health challenges. Mao is a board-certified Family Nurse Practitioner with extensive years of experience in the health industry and has special training in Functional Medicine. She is on a mission to help children be free of chronic health symptoms. It is her belief that every mother should have the know-how of basic holistic practices to better care for her children. She has an online group program that focuses on functional medicine for parents of children with chronic health issues. When not working, she is spending quality time with her husband and 3 daughters. She loves dancing and the outdoors and has taken up gardening as a hobby with the help of her daughters.

www.FionaMao.com

Store: https://fionamao.mindsharecommerce.com

Facebook: https://www.facebook.com/fionamaonp

Instagram: https://www.instagram.com/fionamaonp

Dr. Jordanna Quinn

Physician, Regenerative, Anti-Aging, Functional Medicine, Rehabilitation, Osteopath and Medical Aesthetics

Dr. Jordanna Quinn, D.O, is a board-certified doctor in Physical Medicine and Rehabilitation and has specialty training in Regenerative medicine, Functional medicine, Anti-Aging Medicine and Medical Aesthetics. Dr. Quinn has extensive experience with athletes of all types, professional and amateur.

[1]

Dr. Jordanna Quinn

She enjoys helping busy CEOs, lawyers, doctors and athletes improve their performance, health, and looks so that they can live up to their full potential, without sacrificing their health. Dr. Quinn's extensive training and persistent love of learning enable to her offer an extensive realm of treatments to her patients. She was one of the first physicians in the stem cell space and also one of the first to adopt biohacking as an accepted part of her practice. Dr. Quinn is a true advocate of "practice what you preach". She does not recommend treatments to patients that she would not be willing to do to herself or her family. When Dr. Quinn is not working, she enjoys mountain biking, snowboarding, yoga, and spending time with her family.

www.koremedicine.com

Facebook: https://www.facebook.com/koremedicine

Instagram: https://www.instagram.com/koremedicine

Christi Clemons Hoffman

MA, CHt, Lifelong intuitive, Channel, Teacher, Consultant, and Host of the *Radiate Wellness Podcast* and *Real-Life Angel Encounters Podcast*

PRS Radio Guest of the year Christi Clemons Hoffman is a lifelong intuitive, channel, teacher, and consultant whose passion is connecting people with their spiritual "team." Using a unique blend of Angel Readings, medical intuition, mediumship, and Akashic Records, Christi helps clients with questions about their spiritual growth, unlocking answers to questions about life purpose, past lives, health, relationships, and more.

Christi Clemons Hoffman

Using Reiki techniques along with her intuitive abilities, Christi also helps clients get to the source of physical and emotional discomfort. Christi is also certified at Level 3 in QHHT (Quantum Healing Hypnosis Technique), as developed by Dolores Cannon, one of only 30 Level 3 practitioners in the world. This form of healing works with the Higher Self, or the Subconscious, to discover past lives that have a bearing on the client's current life. It also provides direct communication with the Subconscious, which can scan and heal the body and give the client direction to gain greater understanding, achieve goals, and answer long-held questions.

https://www.radiatewellnesscommunity.com

Facebook: https://www.facebook.com/radiatewellnesskc

Instagram: https://www.instagram.com/radiatewellnesskc